3 p

creative pattern practice

a new approach to writing

MARY E. WHITTEN
North Texas State University

Harcourt, Brace & World, Inc.   New York · Chicago · San Francisco · Atlanta

preface

Creative Pattern Practice: A New Approach to Writing has grown out of the belief that the recent advances in the teaching of foreign languages could profitably be applied to the teaching of the forms and structures of English. The principles of pattern practice, the derivation of rules from examples, the imitation of models, and step-by-step learning are here put to constructive use in an approach that will be new and fresh to students.

The approach to writing in *Creative Pattern Practice* is positive throughout. This text has not one wrong word-form to confuse the student, not one incorrect structure to be revised. Replacing the older techniques are graphic examples of standard usage followed by varied, creative exercises that present, almost incidentally, such important facets of language learning as mechanics, spelling, punctuation, and rhetoric. Instead of selecting between tricky choices, the student uses forms and structures in whole contexts and thus experiences the pleasure of creative achievement.

The book has three main divisions. The four chapters of Part I, "Forms in English," stress word-forms in context, showing their variations by way of specific examples and relating these examples to concise generalizations about standard usage. Numerous exercises provide creative opportunities to put these usage principles into practice. Part II, "Structures in English," stresses groups of words and their relationships to one another, not only in isolated sentences but also in paragraphs. The student first masters the basic sentence structures in English by transforming one acceptable structure into another and then learns to construct well-developed paragraphs through intelligent imitation of a model. In this way he can discover for himself the range of choices that make for effective style. Part III, "A Self-Teaching Review of Grammar," can be taught or used for reference in the classroom, but it has been specifically designed to enable students to assume responsibility for a systematic review of formal grammar on their own.

The author wishes to thank Miss Audrey Ann Welch of Mount Saint Clare College, Clinton, Iowa, for writing many of the exercises, and Professor Gerald Levin of the University of Akron for reading the manuscript and making valuable suggestions.

MARY E. WHITTEN

contents

Preface   v

Part I   **Forms in English**

   1 Agreement   3
       EXERCISES   7
       REVIEW EXERCISES   21

   2 Using Verb Forms   27
       EXERCISES   31
       REVIEW EXERCISES   51

   3 Using Pronouns   57
       EXERCISES   61
       REVIEW EXERCISES   81

   4 Using Modifiers   87
       EXERCISES   89
       REVIEW EXERCISES   99

Part II   **Structures in English**

   1 Phrases and Sentences   105
       REVIEW EXERCISE   183

   2 Paragraphs   187
       REVIEW EXERCISE   201

Part III   **A Self-Teaching Review of Grammar**

   1 Verbs   205
       REVIEW EXERCISES   219

   2 Nouns and Noun Substitutes   223
       REVIEW EXERCISES   241

   3 Modifiers   245
       REVIEW EXERCISES   257

   4 Relators and Expletives   261
       REVIEW EXERCISES   269

Index   273

creative pattern practice
a new approach to writing

part **I**

FORMS IN ENGLISH

1

SINGULAR	PLURAL
Sound moves at various speeds.	*Sounds move* at various speeds.
A *fisherman tells* good stories.	*Fishermen tell* good stories.
With Al *was* a pretty *girl*.	With Al *were* two pretty *girls*.
That does need to be repaired.	*Those do need* to be repaired.
There *has been* no *change*.	There *have been* no *changes*.

A verb changes form to agree grammatically with its subject.

When attached to a subject, the *-s* or *-es* ending indicates plural.

    singular: One *citizen protests*.   The new *church is* open.
    plural: The *citizens protest*.   The new *churches are* open.

When attached to a verb, the *-s* or *-es* ending indicates that (a) the verb is in the present tense and (b) its subject is both singular and in the third person. Compare the subjects of the verbs *work* and *works* below.

    I work, you work, we work, boys work, others work,
    it works, he works, she works, boy works, another works

2

The *stack* of books *has been moved* to the attic.
The crepe paper *streamers* on the car *were* red and white.
Mary Ann, along with her two poodles, now *lives* in France.
Two *articles* in that magazine *deserve* a second reading.

Verbs agree with their subjects, not with objects of prepositions.

3

SINGULAR FORMS ONLY	PLURAL FORMS ONLY
Each was attending school.	Both like steak for breakfast.
Everyone understands him.	Many do not know the score.
Anybody is eligible to join.	Several are rather expensive.
No one has yet volunteered.	A few have quickly withered.

Some pronoun subjects have only one form: singular *or* plural.

These subjects are always singular: *another, each, either, neither, one, no one, everyone, anyone, someone, nobody, everybody, anybody, somebody.*

Everybody in the large class *participates*.
Neither of the steaks *is* tender.
Has either of the ambassadors protested?

These subjects are always plural: *both, few, many, several.*
Note: The number of a few pronouns, such as *all, any, more, most, none,* or *some,* is determined by the word referred to.

Mom baked a *pie*. Some *has* been eaten.

The carpenter left a sack of *nails*. Some *are* bent.

All of the salt *is* damp. *All* of the towels *are* damp.

4a

Leonard and *Bill are* responsible.
Swimming and *golfing appeal* to Dad.
In the bowl *are* a *goldfish* and a *turtle*.
Singular subjects joined by *and* are nearly always plural.

Note: Occasionally, a compound subject is regarded as a single unit and is therefore considered as singular.

The *secretary and reporter* often *arrives* late. (One person arrives late.)
Macaroni and cheese is a good meat substitute. (One dish is.)

4b

Leonard or *Bill is* responsible.
Neither *swimming* nor *golfing appeals* to Dad.
In the bowl *is* a *goldfish* or a *turtle*.
Singular subjects joined by *or* or *nor* remain singular.

Note: If in compound subjects joined by *or* or *nor* one subject is singular and another is plural, the verb agrees with the nearer subject.

Either winds *or hail has* damaged the roof.
Either hail *or winds have* damaged the roof.

5

SINGULAR	PLURAL
There *was* no *variation*.	There *were* no *variations*.
There *is* a *problem* here.	There *are problems* here.
There *has* to be an *answer*.	There *have* to be *answers*.
The expletive *there* has no number and cannot be a subject.	

The expletive *there,* without number and without reference to place, is merely a sentence starter. This introductory *there* can sometimes be omitted, with a shift of word order, in a sentence like the following (and like those in Exercise 7, page 13):

> *There* were two elevators out of order.
> Two elevators were out of order.

In other sentences, such as the one below (and many of those in Exercise 8, page 13), the introductory *there* is more than just a sentence starter because it cannot sensibly be omitted with a shift of word order.

> *There* is scarcely time to catch the train.

Because the expletive *there* occupies the usual subject position, informal English tends to use *is, was, has,* or a similar singular verb form even when the subject is plural. Formal English requires agreement of subject and verb.

6

SINGULAR	PLURAL
This is an *idea that* really *matters.* The *law, which seems* odd, is enforced. Donald is the only *one* of the boys *who knows.*	These are *ideas that* really *matter.* The *laws, which seem* odd, are enforced. Donald is among the *boys who know.*
Antecedents of relative-pronoun subjects determine verb forms.	

7

SINGULAR	PLURAL
The *freshman* had *his* hair cut. *Everybody* did *his* best. A *man* should protect *his* wife. *Neither Tom nor Carl* ever seems to think of *himself.*	The *freshmen* had *their* hair cut. *All* did *their* best. *Men* should protect *their* wives. *Tom and Carl* do not ever seem to think of *themselves.*
Pronouns agree in number with their antecedents.	

An antecedent (which literally means *that which goes before*) is the word to which a pronoun refers:

> *Everyone* should have *his* ticket ready.

Remember that these antecedents are singular: *each, everyone, everybody, anyone, anybody, kind, sort, type, either, neither, one, no one, nobody, man, woman, person.*

Note: A pronoun may clearly refer to an idea rather than to a single antecedent.

This disturbs Simon: *Beelzebub is no ordinary devil.*

EXERCISE 1

All subjects and verbs in this exercise are italicized. Convert each plural subject to singular, each singular subject to plural; then make the verb agree. Do not shift the tense of the verb.

A. *Scientists ask* questions.   A <u>scientist asks</u> questions.

B. *Has* there *been* any *call?*   <u>Have</u> there been any <u>calls?</u>

1. Free *men resist* tyranny.   A free _____ tyranny.

2. *Does* the *boy understand?*   _____ the _____ understand?

3. The *artists start* fads.   The _____ fads.

4. All *members get* some keys.   Every _____ some keys.

5. There *goes* the *official.*   There _____ the _____.

6. Here *are* clever *ideas.*   Here _____ a clever _____.

7. Where *is* the show *ticket?*   Where _____ the show _____?

8. Behind me *was* a *truck.*   Behind me _____ two _____.

9. *Dentists risk* infection.   A _____ infection.

10. *Has* the *horse been* sold?   _____ the _____ been sold?

EXERCISE 2

Oral Drill: Read the following sentences aloud, carefully pronouncing the correct italicized verbs and subjects.

1. Sudden *shifts* often *cause* trouble. Sudden *shifts* in policy often *cause* trouble.

2. The *windows seem* adequate. The *windows* in the office *seem* adequate.

3. Many a *freshman wastes* time. Many a *freshman* with poor work habits *wastes* time.

4. The *putty shows* under the paint. The *putty* in those nail holes *shows* under the paint.

5. The *man has* worries. The *man* with a wife and children *has* worries.

6. Not *many know* how to fence. Not *many* in the class *know* how to fence.

7. *Everyone is* invited. Every *one* of you *is* invited.

EXERCISE 3

Using the preposition given in parentheses, change each italicized word below to a subject followed by a prepositional phrase; then complete the sentence, making sure that the verb agrees with the subject. Do not change the tense of the verb. Follow the pattern of the examples.

A. The factory *workers* have called off the strike.

(at) _____ The workers at the factory have called off the strike. _____

B. Has *either* bid been accepted?

(of) _____ Has either of the bids been accepted? _____

1. Greenville *streets* are both rough and narrow.

(in) _____

2. *One* wrestler has fallen through the ropes.

(of) _____

3. Stage *whispers* are sometimes directed to the prompter.

(on) _____

4. Does *either* driver accept the blame for the accident?

(of) _____

5. Spring *romances* do not always lead to the altar.

(during) _____

6. The St. Louis *teams* are leading in the tournament.

(from) _____

7. *Each* screen needs painting.

(of) _____

8. The highway *signs* are especially attractive.

(along) _____

9. Doesn't *either* program keep your family interested?

(of) _____

10. *One* player was injured during the first half of the game.

(of) _____

EXERCISE 4

Oral Drill: Read the following correct sentences aloud, stressing the italicized words. If a sentence sounds wrong to you, read it aloud several times.

1. *Both* of my parents *were* notified.

2. *Neither* of my parents *was* notified.

3. *Do many* of the courses *deal* with current problems?

4. *Does either* of the courses *deal* with current problems?

5. A *few* in my class *speak* Spanish.

6. *No one* in my class *speaks* Spanish.

7. *Nobody* on the stage *remembers* the lines.

8. *Several* on the stage *remember* the lines.

9. *Each* of these poems *has* vivid figures of speech.

10. *Everyone* in the stadium *stands* up and *cheers* for Randy.

EXERCISE 5

For each singular subject below, use *is* as the verb (or as part of the verb); for each plural subject, use *are* as the verb (or as part of the verb). Complete each thought, writing a grammatically complete sentence.

A. Each of those pens _is leaking._____

B. Several of the boys in the dormitory _are on the team._____

1. Each of his friends _____

2. Both of them _____

3. No one in the room _____

4. Every one of you _____

5. Neither of your uncles _____

6. Anybody in the crowd _____

7. A few in the gymnasium _____

8. Everybody in the smoker _____

9. Both of those tennis rackets _____

10. Several of the sports writers _____

EXERCISE 6

Oral and written drill: (a) Read each of the following questions aloud, stressing the correct italicized words. (b) Using compound subjects joined by the conjunctions given in parentheses, answer each question. Do not change the tense of the verb; make sure that the verb agrees with its subject.

A. *Do Brian and Merle* take voice lessons?

(neither—nor) _____ Neither Brian nor Merle takes them._____

B. *Is Kokomo or Wabash* located in Indiana?

(both—and) _____ Both Kokomo and Wabash are._____

1. *Does John or Robert* own a sailboat?

   (neither—nor) _____

2. *Has he or Larry* ever been to a world's fair?

   (and) _____

3. *Is punctuality or attendance* especially important?

   (and) _____

4. *Have* the *money and* the *wallet* been returned?

   (neither—nor) _____

5. *Was coffee or tea* served at the break?

   (both—and) _____

6. *Have she and Carl* ever been in a play before?

   (neither—nor) _____

7. *Are Frank and Joe* lying about the theft?

   (either—or) _____

8. *Were* the *door and* the *window* open?

   (or) _____

9. *Is* a *tie,* a *book,* or a *bouquet* an appropriate gift?

   (and) _____

10. *Were* the *author and* his *wife* waiting at the airport?

    (neither—nor) _____

EXERCISE 7

Revise the correct sentences below by using the expletive *there* to begin each sentence. Be sure that each verb agrees with its subject; do not change the tense of the verb.

    A. Several policemen were at the scene.

    <u>There were several policemen</u> at the scene.

    B. Many reforms have been introduced.

    <u>There have been many reforms</u> introduced.

1. Books and clothes were lying everywhere.

    _____ everywhere.

2. A jet is circling the airport.

    _____ circling the airport.

3. An excellent speech was given at the convention.

    _____ at the convention.

4. A great many actors were out of work.

    _____ out of work.

5. No theater tickets are available.

    _____ available.

EXERCISE 8

After determining the number of the subject of each sentence below, correctly fill in each blank with either *There was* or *There were*.

1. _____ eight curtain calls.

2. _____ a total eclipse of the sun.

3. _____ three or four letters.

4. _____ hardly enough money to take the trip.

5. _____ no definite solution to Jack's problem.

6. _____ good reasons for Odysseus' delay.

7. _____ fantastic price reductions.

8. _____ rivers which served as highways.

9. _____ a one-cent sale on ball-point pens.

10. _____ few opportunities to advance.

11. _____ scarcely any encouragement.

12. _____ free samples for regular customers.

13. _____ good trout-fishing in the mountain streams.

14. _____ nicknames for nearly all the freshmen.

15. _____ a few fire-prevention posters.

16. _____ too many demands to meet.

17. _____ no way to ship natural gas except by pipe.

18. _____ no plans to cancel the track meet.

19. _____ acrobats of marvelous dexterity.

20. _____ five chances in a hundred that Penelope would

finish the robe.

Name _____ Section _____ Date _____

EXERCISE 9

Using the relative-pronoun subjects given in parentheses, fill in the blanks according to the pattern of the example. Do not shift the tense of the verbs.

Ed played his favorite record. It was a ballad.   (which)

a. Ed played his favorite record, which was a ballad.

b. Ed played his favorite records, which were ballads.

1. I know his cousin. He is a famous architect.   (who)

a. I know his cousin, _____

b. I know his cousins, _____

2. I bought the more expensive watch. It was waterproof.   (which)

a. I bought the more expensive watch, _____

b. I bought the more expensive watches, _____

3. Grandfather says no. He is afraid of change.   (who)

a. Grandfather, _____, says no.

b. My grandparents, _____, say no.

4. Bruce intends to visit his aunt. She does not know his plans as yet.   (who)

a. Bruce intends to visit his aunt, _____

_____

b. Bruce intends to visit his aunts, _____

_____

5. I'll ask the bell captain. He knows the city well.   (who)

a. I'll ask the bell captain, _____

b. I'll ask the bell boys, _____

EXERCISE 10

Convert each of the following according to the pattern of the example.

Only Fred smokes cigars. The other boys do not.   (who)

Fred is the only one of those boys <u>who smokes cigars.</u>

1. Only Bob thinks independently. The other young men do not.   (who)

   Bob is the only one of the young men _____

   _____

2. Only Grandma dips snuff. My other relatives do not.   (who)

   Grandma is the only one of my relatives _____

   _____

3. Only Rusty bites our postman. The other dogs do not.   (that)

   Rusty is the only one of the dogs _____

   _____

4. Only the science building is new. The other buildings are not.   (that)

   The science building is the only one of the buildings _____

   _____

5. Only music interests Jim. Other arts do not.   (that)

   Music is the only one of the arts _____

   _____

EXERCISE 11

Combine the following pairs of sentences according to the pattern of the example.

> Many plays have been presented on our campus. *The Miracle Worker* is one of the best of them. (that)
>
> *The Miracle Worker* is one of the best plays that have been presented on our campus.

1. Many characters appear in *The Canterbury Tales*. Griselda is one of the more insipid of these characters. (who)

   Griselda is one of the more insipid characters _____

   _____

2. Some people just do not understand Tony. Clarence is one of those people. (who)

   Clarence is one of those people _____

   _____

3. Some countries have summer in December, January, and February. Chile is one of these countries. (that)

   Chile is one of the countries _____

   _____

4. Several birds resemble the stork. An adjutant is one of these birds. (that)

   An adjutant is one of several birds _____

   _____

5. Many suburban lots are likely to double in value. This lot is one of them. (that)

   This is one of those suburban lots _____

   _____

6. Some tourists have traveled far but have seen little. Walter acts like one of those tourists. (who)

   Walter acts like one of those tourists _____

   _____

7. Some women have no interest but fashion. Annette dresses like one of those women. (who)

   Annette dresses like one of those women _____

   _____

8. A few boys ask for more porridge. Oliver is one of those boys. (who)

   Oliver is one of the boys _____

9. Some TV shows appeal to practically all Americans. The six o'clock news is one of these TV shows. (that)

   The six o'clock news is one of the TV shows _____

   _____

10. Those girls are giving away jeweled pipes. Terry is one of those girls. (who)

    Terry is one of those girls _____

    _____

EXERCISE 12

Correctly fill in each blank below by using either *his* or *their* to agree with the number of the antecedent.

1. May all passengers bring _____ pets aboard?

2. May every passenger bring _____ pets aboard?

3. Many men are prone to follow _____ own hunches.

4. That type of man is prone to follow _____ own hunches.

5. Every member forgot to bring _____ copy of the constitution.

6. Everybody forgot to bring _____ copy of the constitution.

7. All members can offer _____ suggestions.

8. Anyone can offer _____ suggestions.

9. Many of the boys brought _____ own food.

10. No one brought _____ own food.

11. Everybody brought _____ own food.

12. Visitors may not take _____ cameras there.

13. A visitor may not take _____ camera there.

14. Nobody on the tour can take _____ camera there.

15. Both Tony and Herbert can sign _____ own checks.

16. Tony and Herbert can sign _____ own checks.

17. Both can sign _____ own checks.

18. Either can sign _____ own checks.

19. All the waiters hurried to collect _____ tips.

20. Each waiter hurried to collect _____ tips.

Name _____ Section _____ Date _____

REVIEW EXERCISE A

Correctly fill in the blanks with the verbs specified.

Use *was* or *were*.

1. A half dollar and a dime _____ lying on the counter.

2. There _____ several keys in the top desk drawer.

3. On the table _____ stacks of magazines.

4. Only a few of the roses _____ left on the bush.

5. Both of those streams _____ good for trout-fishing.

6. Each of the debates _____ thought-provoking.

Use *has* or *have*.

7. Several of the machines _____ worn out.

8. There _____ been few losses this year.

9. Either he or Sam _____ already made reservations.

10. Many signs of unrest _____ appeared.

11. Where _____ Mr. Ames and his friends gone?

12. It is one of those cottages that _____ no fireplace.

13. There _____ been many volunteers for the work.

14. Neither Lucy nor her brother _____ any money left.

Use *do* or *does*.

15. _____ every one of them understand?

16. Not one of them _____ understand.

agreement 21

17. Frank is the only one of the singers who _____ remember all the words to the melody.

18. There _____ not appear to be any quick answers.

19. Ask one of the mechanics who _____ know how.

20. Recently discovered facts about the language of dolphins _____ interest Dr. Thomas, a linguist.

REVIEW EXERCISE B

After choosing a suitable verb *in the present tense* for each subject below, complete each sentence.

1. Each of my fraternity brothers _____

2. Both of the capsules in the bottle _____

3. Lou and her best friend _____

4. Neither Samuel nor his wife _____

5. Sam, like his friends, _____

6. Neither of the professors _____

7. A few of the professors _____

8. Everyone in the mob _____

9. All of the freshmen _____

10. Nobody in the large audience _____

11. Many among the crowd _____

12. Either he or Ted _____

13. He and Ted _____

14. Apple trees all along the lane _____

15. Women at the political meeting _____

16. Everybody on the team _____

17. Several on the team _____

18. No one on the team _____

19. Marvin is one of the players who _____

_____

20. Marvin is the only one of the players who _____

_____

_Name _____ Section _____ Date _____

REVIEW EXERCISE C

Fill in the spaces by changing the verbs and pronouns (and the nouns when necessary) to make them agree with the changed subjects (their antecedents). Do not shift the verb tenses.

   A. Each scout has the time of his life.

     Many scouts _have the time of their lives._ _____

   B. Statesmen dedicate themselves to the service of their country.

     A statesman _dedicates himself to the service of his country._ _____

1. A young husband encourages his wife to learn to cook.

   Young husbands _____

2. The seniors were eager to get their diplomas.

   Each senior _____

3. All the Spartan boys were rigorously trained to do their duty.

   Every Spartan boy _____

_____

4. Each article in the window is marked far below its value.

   All articles in the window _____

_____

5. Freshmen occasionally consider themselves overworked.

   Every freshman occasionally _____

6. Too often wives find excuses for their own failures.

   Too often a wife _____

7. The youngest of Lear's daughters declares her love for her father.

   All three of Lear's daughters _____

_____

8. Jude appreciates your thanks for his thoughtfulness.

Jude and Jane _____

9. People are inclined at times to magnify their own faults.

A person _____

_____

10. Hunters in these mountains tip liberally because they know the value of their native guides.

A hunter in these mountains _____

_____

using verb forms 2

1

He *asked* Catherine.	Lives *will be risked.*
It *has happened* before.	*Are* we *being criticized?*
Had she *talked* to you?	I *have been advised* otherwise.

The -*d* and -*ed* forms of regular verbs are used (a) for the simple past tense, (b) with *have*, *has*, and *had*, and (c) with forms of *be*.

Use and *suppose* have the past form when *used to* is roughly equivalent to *did* and when *supposed to* means *expected to*.

> David *used to* walk a great deal. (David did walk . . . .)
> I am *supposed to* be there early. (I am expected to be . . . .)

2

-*ing* VERBS	PASSIVE VERBS
A tenor *is singing* the aria.	The aria *is sung* by a tenor.
Were you *laughing* at them?	*Were* they *being laughed* at?
He *has been stretching* facts.	The facts *have been stretched.*

In verb phrases, forms of *be* act as auxiliaries (a) with -*ing* verbs and (b) with past participles to form the passive voice.

There are eight forms of *be: am, is, are, was, were, be, been, being.* To be a part of the verb phrase in a sentence, an -*ing* verb form must have with it an appropriate form of *be*.

> *verb phrase in a sentence:* Jan *was leaving* it up to me.
> *fragment (no verb):* Jan *leaving* it up to me

A passive verb phrase must always include a form of *be*.

> *passive verb phrase in a sentence:* Words *were spoken* in anger.
> *fragment (no verb):* words *spoken* in anger

3

INFINITIVE FORM	SIMPLE PAST	PAST PARTICIPLE
Break the seal.	You *broke* the seal.	I have *broken* it.
Dad will *drive*.	Dad *drove* fast.	My car was *driven*.
He won't *eat* it.	He finally *ate* it.	He has *eaten* it.
Snow might *fall*.	Snow *fell* in May.	Snow had *fallen*.
Jack may *fly* there.	Jack *flew* there.	Has Jack *flown*?
Did you *freeze* it?	You *froze* me out.	The meat is *frozen*.
I often *give* up.	I often *gave* up.	I've *given* up.
She should *know* it.	She *knew* it.	Is it *known* yet?
Hal is to *speak* now.	Hal *spoke* too long.	Has he *spoken* here?
We'll *take* turns.	We *took* turns.	We had *taken* turns.
Does he *wear* size 8?	He *wore* his tuxedo.	Had he *worn* a coat?
Pete used to *write*.	Pete *wrote* fiction.	Notes will be *written*.

The simple-past verb forms never have verb helpers or auxiliaries.

When an *-n* or *-en* verb form is the principal verb, one of these auxiliaries must accompany it: *has, have, had,* or a form of *be.*

Note: Sometimes *get* (or *got*) functions as an auxiliary which is equivalent to *be* (or *was* or *were*).

> The notes *will get written.* (The notes will be written.)
> The notes *got written.* (The notes were written.)

4

INFINITIVE FORM	SIMPLE PAST	PAST PARTICIPLE
You never *do* that.	You never *did* that.	That was never *done*.
I ought to *go* now.	I *went* to bed.	I had *gone* to bed.
Alma will *see* them.	Alma *saw* them then.	Has Alma *seen* them?

Did, went, and *saw* never have verb helpers or auxiliaries.

When *done, gone,* or *seen* is the principal verb, one of these auxiliaries must accompany it: *has, have, had,* or a form of *be.*

5

INFINITIVE FORM	SIMPLE PAST	PAST PARTICIPLE
Begin immediately.	The rains *began*.	The rains have *begun*.
I *drink* the milk.	I *drank* the milk.	The milk has been *drunk*.
We shall *swim*.	We *swam* there.	We have *swum* there.

Began, drank, and *swam* never have verb helpers or auxiliaries.

When *begun, drunk,* or *swum* is the principal verb, one of these auxiliaries must accompany it: *has, have, had,* or a form of *be.*

6

INFINITIVE FORM	SIMPLE PAST	PAST PARTICIPLE
Come home now.	Paula *came* home.	Paula has *come* home.
I may *run* away.	Yesterday I *ran* away.	I had *run* away.
The verb forms *came* and *ran* are never used with auxiliaries.		

The infinitive form of *come* and *run* is the same as the past participle. A form of *have* (*has, have, had*) or a form of *be* must always be used with the past participle.

7

INFINITIVE FORM	PRESENT PARTICIPLE	SIMPLE PAST	PAST PARTICIPLE
set	setting	set	set
lay	laying	laid	laid

ACTIVE VOICE (WITH OBJECTS)	PASSIVE VOICE
I *used to set* the pace.	The pace *used to be set* by me.
They *lay* carpets.	Carpets *are laid* by that company.
He *is setting* her hair.	Her hair *was being set*.
We *have set* up the rules.	The rules *have been set* up.
He *has been laying* bricks.	The bricks *have been laid*.

Ordinarily, forms of *set* and *lay* either have objects or are used (with a form of *be*) in the passive voice.

8

INFINITIVE FORM	PRESENT PARTICIPLE	SIMPLE PAST	PAST PARTICIPLE
sit	sitting	sat	sat
lie	lying	lay	lain

I *ought to sit* down.	I *ought to lie* down.
My dog *is sitting* near me.	My dog *is lying* near me.
An hour ago I *sat* down.	An hour ago I *lay* down.
Have you *sat* here very long?	*Have* you *lain* here very long?

Forms of *sit* and *lie* do not have objects and are not passive.

9

INDICATIVE MOOD	SUBJUNCTIVE MOOD
Paul *is* not a genius.	She wishes Paul *were* a genius.
I *am* not you.	If I *were* you, I would quit.
He often *sees* the dean.	I suggest that he *see* the dean.
They *should be fired*.	I demand that they *be fired*.

Verb forms in the subjunctive mood are used (a) for wishes, (b) for expressions contrary to fact, and (c) in clauses that follow such words as *suggest, demand, urge,* and *recommend.*

Name _____ Section _____ Date _____

EXERCISE 1

Following the pattern below, answer each of the questions in the affirmative.

Did someone drown here?   Yes, someone drowned here. _____

1. Did enemies attack? _____

2. Did that really happen? _____

3. Did she ask Mr. Waters? _____

4. Did they surprise you? _____

5. Did he walk down? _____

6. Did Joe risk his life? _____

7. Did they refuse to act? _____

8. Did they laugh today? _____

9. Did the child drown? _____

10. Did he advise that? _____

EXERCISE 2

Change each *did* below to *used to,* and each *expected to* to *supposed to.*

A. I did cry.   I used to cry. _____

B. He is expected to speak.   He is supposed to speak. _____

1. I did hunt often. _____

2. I am expected to go now. _____

3. You did play fair. _____

4. You are expected to play fair. _____

using verb forms   31

5. We did go crayfishing. _____

6. We were expected to pay our share. _____

7. Dad did plant beans here. _____

8. Dad was expected to be there early. _____

9. I did have patience. _____

10. You are expected to lead. _____

EXERCISE 3

Change the italicized word to the subject. Use the *-d* or *-ed* form of the regular verb with (a) *was* or *were*, (b) *has been* or *have been*, (c) *will be*, and (d) *had been*.

Ask *questions.*

a. _Questions were asked._   c. _Questions will be asked._

b. _Questions have been asked._   d. _Questions had been asked._

1. Stamp the *cards.*

a. _____   c. _____

b. _____   d. _____

2. Italicize the *titles.*

a. _____   c. _____

b. _____   d. _____

3. Guess the *answers.*

a. _____   c. _____

b. _____   d. _____

4. Help your *neighbor.*

a. _____   c. _____

b. _____   d. _____

5. Form *lines.*

a. _____   c. _____

b. _____   d. _____

6. Carve a *model.*

    a. _____   c. _____

    b. _____   d. _____

7. Open the *window.*

    a. _____   c. _____

    b. _____   d. _____

8. Solve the *puzzle.*

    a. _____   c. _____

    b. _____   d. _____

9. Pursue that *idea.*

    a. _____   c. _____

    b. _____   d. _____

10. Arrange the *flight.*

    a. _____   c. _____

    b. _____   d. _____

EXERCISE 4

Following the pattern below, convert the fragments to sentences by using the auxiliaries given in parentheses.

A. (was) *My father was being entirely too indifferent.*

B. (have been) *Supplies have been not yet dealt out to flood victims.*

C. (has been) *The cub plane has been sold but not delivered.*

1. (were) the girls wondering about Fred's reaction

2. (have been) all my important chemistry notes lost

3. (has been) legislative action not concerned with reform

4. (was) a Mexican basket bought in San Antonio

5. (are) horses led to the track early in the morning

6. (may be) good resolutions thought about but never carried out

7. (am) I sending out wedding invitations and writing thank-you notes for early gifts

8. (had been) diving helmets used by sportsmen in the 1940's

9. (are) dams not only conserving water but also controlling floods

10. (have been) several books lent but none returned

11. (was) wall-to-wall nylon carpeting laid in our living room last Saturday

12. (is) Tommy acting so spoiled that no one wants to be around him

13. (are) coins tossed into the fountain every day by wistful tourists

14. (had been) Christians using the catacombs as shelters from persecutions and as burial grounds

15. (were) the last words of the jet pilot not heard

16. (was)   one of those fly balls caught during the first inning

17. (were)   brick apartment houses built in northern Italy

18. (had been)   the telephone not yet connected, and Dad was pleased

19. (has been)   violent wind lashing the Atlantic coast all week

20. (has been)   the Atlantic coast lashed all week by violent wind

EXERCISE 5

Convert each phrase below into two sentences according to the pattern of the examples.

A. broken glass _Somebody broke the glass. It was broken._

B. apples eaten _Somebody ate the apples. They were eaten._

1. broken mirror

_____

2. nails driven

_____

3. frozen okra

_____

4. given account

_____

5. known facts

_____

6. written replies

_____

7. worn shoes

_____

8. jets flown

_____

9. vows taken

_____

10. spoken lines

_____

EXERCISE 6

Answer the questions below, using the structural pattern and verb tenses of the examples.

A. Were they breaking up?

_____They broke up. They had broken up before._____

B. Were they writing it?

_____They wrote it. They had written it before._____

1. Were they giving up?

_____

2. Were they taking it?

_____

3. Were they wearing them?

_____

4. Were they speaking up?

_____

5. Were they freezing it?

_____

6. Were they flying?

_____

7. Were they falling?

_____

8. Were they driving?

_____

9. Were they writing him?

_____

10. Were they eating?

_____

EXERCISE 7

Fill in the blanks by using correct forms (other than *-ing* forms) of the italicized verbs.

go	*do*	*see*
A. has not _gone_	has not _done_	has not _seen_
B. last year I _went_	last year I _did_	last year I _saw_
1. may _____	may _____	may _____
2. has not _____	has not _____	has not _____
3. yesterday I _____	yesterday I _____	yesterday I _____
4. will have _____	will have _____	will have _____
5. last week he _____	last week he _____	last week he _____
6. have _____	have _____	have _____
7. had often _____	had often _____	had often _____
8. would have _____	would have _____	would have _____
9. have once _____	have once _____	have once _____
10. could be _____	could be _____	could be _____

EXERCISE 8

Fill in the blanks by using correct forms (other than -ing forms) of the italicized verbs.

begin	*swim*	*drink*
A. was not begun	was not swum	was not drunk
B. last week he began	last week he swam	last week he drank
1. we had _____	we had _____	we had _____
2. shall be _____	shall be _____	shall be _____
3. last year I _____	last year I_____	last year I _____
4. have not _____	have not _____	have not _____
5. has been _____	has been _____	has been _____
6. were never _____	were never _____	were never _____
7. last year he _____	last year he _____	last year he _____
8. she had _____	she had _____	she had _____
9. could be _____	could be _____	could be _____
10. may have been _____	may have been _____	may have been _____

EXERCISE 9

Give the corresponding forms of the italicized verbs, following the pattern of the examples.

swim	*drink*	*begin*
A. Did Jan swim?	Did Jan drink?	Did Jan begin?
B. Have you swum it?	Have you drunk it?	Have you begun it?
C. He swam today.	He drank today.	He began today.

1. Was it swum? _____ _____

2. _____ Will it be drunk? _____

3. _____ _____ He will begin soon.

4. Had he swum? _____ _____

5. _____ I drank that. _____

6. _____ _____ Will we begin?

7. He doesn't swim. _____ _____

8. _____ Can it be drunk? _____

9. _____ _____ It was begun.

10. They never swam. _____ _____

EXERCISE 10

Following the pattern of the examples, write sentences with appropriate forms of *come* and *run*. Do not shift tense.

A. Afterward we went home.

   a. Afterward we came home. _____

   b. Afterward we ran home. _____

B. He had dashed to her rescue.

   a. He had come to her rescue. _____

   b. He had run to her rescue. _____

1. They had already sailed away.

   a. _____

   b. _____

2. We skidded round the corner.

   a. _____

   b. _____

3. Has the train always left on time?

   a. _____

   b. _____

4. Later the crowd rushed in.

   a. _____

   b. _____

5. Several players limped off the field.

   a. _____

b. _____

6. He jumped across it.

    a. _____

    b. _____

7. The rain poured down the walls.

    a. _____

    b. _____

8. Have your brothers gone yet?

    a. _____

    b. _____

9. I had already turned back.

    a. _____

    b. _____

10. Lucy flew over to see you.

    a. _____

    b. _____

EXERCISE 11

Transform each phrase below into sentences, following the pattern of the examples.

A. a set table   <u>Set a table.</u>   <u>A table was set.</u>

B. laid plans   <u>Lay plans.</u>   <u>Plans were laid.</u>

1. a set value   _____   _____

2. a set course   _____   _____

3. a set place   _____   _____

4. set alarms   _____   _____

5. a set time   _____   _____

6. laid cement   _____   _____

7. laid dust   _____   _____

8. laid bets   _____   _____

9. laid tile   _____   _____

10. a laid cable   _____   _____

EXERCISE 12

Following the pattern of the examples, change the verbs to appropriate forms of *set* and *lay*. Do not shift tense.

A. She puts empty boxes on this shelf.

   a. <u>She sets empty boxes on this shelf.</u>

   b. <u>She lays empty boxes on this shelf.</u>

B. Since then, I have thrown bent nails aside.

   a.   Since then, I have set bent nails aside.

   b.   Since then, I have laid bent nails aside.

1. Finally I fixed the trap.

   a. _____

   b. _____

2. Put those books on my desk.

   a. _____

   b. _____

3. The scraps of lumber were stored here.

   a. _____

   b. _____

4. Ann was putting the silverware at the places.

   a. _____

   b. _____

5. I have displayed the gift on my desk.

   a. _____

   b. _____

EXERCISE 13

Following the patterns below, fill in the blanks by using appropriate forms of *sit* and *lie*. Do not shift tense.

A. Where was he resting?

a. Where was he sitting? _____

b. Where was he lying? _____

B. Luke sometimes remains there an hour.

a. Luke sometimes sits there an hour. _____

b. Luke sometimes lies there an hour. _____

1. We boys were relaxing on the beach.

a. _____

b. _____

2. I stood still for a moment.

a. _____

b. _____

3. The mallard decoy has stayed there for days.

a. _____

b. _____

4. Meanwhile she swung in the hammock.

a. _____

b. _____

5. Joe had waited there at least an hour.

a. _____

b. _____

6. I may be reading under the shade tree.

   a. _____

   b. _____

7. Henry's terrier sleeps in that chair.

   a. _____

   b. _____

8. Mimi fell in a patch of gravel.

   a. _____

   b. _____

9. Please do not stay there another minute.

   a. _____

   b. _____

10. Will that lazy boy be hammering on the roof today?

   a. _____

   b. _____

EXERCISE 14

Use the subjunctive mood to form a new sentence derived from each pair of sentences below; follow the pattern of the examples.

A. Shubert makes wishes. He wants to be an astronaut.

Shubert wishes he were an astronaut.

B. I am not you. But I think you should resign.

If I were you, I would resign.

C. I insist upon it. He must do a good job.

I insist that he do a good job.

1. Jim often makes a wish. He wants to be an acrobat.

2. I am not Ralph. But I think he should marry.

3. Mr. Carter requests it. The applicant must be over twenty.

4. The roof is not leaking. Otherwise it would be repaired.

5. He is not a good driver. Otherwise I would let him use my car.

6. It is not possible. Otherwise the meeting would be adjourned.

7. The board recommends it. The prisoner should go free.

8. Cynthia makes wishes. She wants to be a TV star.

_____

9. I demand this. She must explain.

_____

10. Ellen is not Joe. But she thinks he should join the Peace Corps.

_____

REVIEW EXERCISE A

Change verb forms below according to the pattern of the examples.

A. Did he run?

   He ran. He has run before. _____

B. Did he eat it?

   He ate it. He has eaten it before. _____

1. Did he begin?

   _____

2. Did he ask?

   _____

3. Did he attack?

   _____

4. Did he see it?

   _____

5. Did he drink it?

   _____

6. Did he grasp it?

   _____

7. Did he speak?

   _____

8. Did he fly it?

   _____

9. Did he give it?

_____

10. Did he go?

_____

11. Did he come?

_____

12. Did he take it?

_____

13. Did he fall?

_____

14. Did he wear it?

_____

15. Did he swim?

_____

REVIEW EXERCISE B

Fill in the blank with the correct form of the verb in parentheses.

A. (sit)   We have __sat_____ in the balcony several times.

B. (use)   We __used_____ to like square dancing.

1. (ask)   Yesterday I _____ a foolish question.

2. (sit)   Please _____ down and rest a few minutes.

3. (lie)   The books are _____ on the floor.

4. (lay)   The books were _____ on the floor.

5. (begin)   Has the waltz _____?

6. (do)   I _____ it before he arrived.

7. (drink)   Have you ever _____ watermelon juice?

8. (eat)   All the refreshments were _____ quickly.

9. (wear)   Has she ever _____ a formal dress before?

10. (drive)   George has never _____ a jeep.

11. (fall)   Not all of the leaves have _____ yet.

12. (write)   Have you _____ to Mr. Clayton yet?

13. (run)   Last week he _____ twenty yards for a score.

14. (take)   Has she _____ the qualifying examination?

15. (swim)   Last summer we _____ in the Pacific Ocean.

16. (speak)   Not one unkind word was _____.

17. (see)   Never had I _____ such fireworks!

18. (lie)   Yesterday toys _____ all over the hall.

19. (come)   Last Monday my brother _____ back.

20. (go)   Have they _____ to the library?

21. (suppose)   We are _____ to be there on time.

22. (give)   Yesterday my uncle _____ me ten dollars.

23. (be)   If I _____ you, I would not give up.

24. (know)   Very little is _____ about the new drug.

25. (freeze)   The ornamental pepper plants had _____.

REVIEW EXERCISE C

If a verb listed below is an infinitive form or a simple-past form (never used with *has, have, had,* or a form of *be*), write *X* in the blank. If the verb is a past-participle form (used with *has, have, had,* or a form of *be*), write *have* in the blank.

A. ___X___ drink   B. ___have___ swum   C. ___X___ took

1. _____ begun
2. _____ lay
3. _____ came
4. _____ ask
5. _____ done
6. _____ drank
7. _____ swam
8. _____ begin
9. _____ taken
10. _____ advise
11. _____ spoke
12. _____ give
13. _____ known
14. _____ broke
15. _____ fell
16. _____ ran
17. _____ drunk

18. _____ did
19. _____ went
20. _____ seen
21. _____ wrote
22. _____ drove
23. _____ flew
24. _____ saw
25. _____ lain
26. _____ wore
27. _____ froze
28. _____ began
29. _____ attack
30. _____ lie
31. _____ broken
32. _____ driven
33. _____ written
34. _____ sang

using pronouns 3

1

SUBJECTS	SUBJECT COMPLEMENTS
He and *I* agreed.	Yes, it was *she*.
We paid more than *they*.	It might be *he* or Jones.
Who made that mistake?	That is *she* sitting by Neal.

The pronouns *I, he, she, we, they, who,* and *whoever* are used as subjects of verbs and as subject complements.

I, he, she, we, they, who, and *whoever* function as subjects and subject complements not only in simple sentences and in main clauses but also in subordinate clauses:

SUBJECTS	SUBJECT COMPLEMENTS
I hope *he and Tom will go.*	I know *it must be he.*
Send it to *whoever needs it.*	You can guess *who it is.*
Who do you think *lost?*	Come in, *whoever you are.*

Some writers avoid pronoun complements which may seem awkward or stilted. For instance, these writers may use "*He* deserves to win!" instead of "It is *he* who deserves to win!"

Notice the differences between formal and informal usage of pronoun complements:

> *formal:*   It is I. It is he. It is they.
> *informal:* It's me. It's him. It's them.

2

OBJECTS OF VERBS	OBJECTS OF PREPOSITIONS
He will not forget *them* or *us*.	She sat between *him* and *me*.
Dad sent Bill and *me* money.	Everyone except *her* obeyed.
Will Rogers liked *whomever* he met.	"Ask not for *whom* the bell tolls," Donne advises.

The pronouns *me, him, her, us, them, whom,* and *whomever* are used as objects of verbs and as objects of prepositions.

Formal usage requires *whom* as an object form. Informal usage, however, calls for *who* rather than *whom* as the natural way to begin or end a question, regardless of grammatical structure. In conversational English, *whom* might well disappear, were it not used occasionally after a preposition.

> *formal:*   To *whom* is the mayor writing? Who outplayed *whom?*
> *informal:* Who is the mayor writing to? Who outplayed *who?*

3

SUBJECTS OF INFINITIVES	OBJECTS OF INFINITIVES
Mother expects *me* to marry. I watched *her* and *him* dive. *Whom* did he want to do it?	Cleve expects to marry *me*. He made Vi pay *them* and *us*. You know *whom* to ask first.

The pronouns *me, him, her, us, them,* and *whom* function as subjects of infinitives and as objects of infinitives.

4

SUBJECT PRONOUNS	OBJECT PRONOUNS
Al paid Sue more than *we*. Al paid Sue more than *we* did. Ed likes Ann as well as *I*. Ed likes Ann as well as *I* do.	Al paid Sue more than *us*. Al paid Sue more than he paid *us*. Ed likes Ann as well as *me*. Ed likes Ann as well as he likes *me*.

The choice of subject or object pronouns after *than* or *as* depends upon their use in the subordinate clause.

5

SUBJECT FORMS AS APPOSITIVES	OBJECT FORMS AS APPOSITIVES
The younger *boys*—*he* and Ron— waited for an hour. It was our two *guests, she* and Perry. *We* girls—both you and *I*—must go now.	We waited for the younger *boys*—*him* and Ron. They brought along two *guests, her* and Perry. Let's you and *me* go to the box office now.

The choice of subject or object pronoun forms for appositives depends upon the use of the words identified or explained.

Appositives can take the place of the words identified or explained:

> Give *us*—John and *me*—more time.
> Give John and me more time.

An appositive which follows a pronoun does not affect the pronoun form:

> *We* will help. *We boys* will help.
> Please help *us*. Please help *us girls*.

6

POSSESSIVE FORMS SUBSTITUTING FOR NOUNS	POSSESSIVE FORMS MODIFYING NOUNS AND GERUNDS
I appreciate not only John's help but also *yours*. *Theirs* are taller and sturdier than *ours*.	I appreciate *your* help. I appreciate *your* helping me. *Their* clipping the hedges disturbs *our* whole family.

The possessive pronouns *mine, yours, his, hers, ours, theirs,* and *whose* act as one-word substitutes for a possessive plus its noun. The possessive pronouns *my, your, his, her, its, our, their,* and *whose* modify nouns or noun substitutes (gerunds).

Do not confuse contractions with possessive pronouns. Possessive pronouns do not have apostrophes.

CONTRACTIONS	POSSESSIVE PRONOUNS
It's knocking.	The motor continued *its* knocking.
They're right.	I question *their* right to do this.
There's no danger.	*Theirs* is not dangerous.
You're happy.	*Your* happiness is important.
Who's here?	*Whose* is it?

7

SINGULAR	PLURAL
A *man* should support **himself**. *Everybody* planned **his** future. Did *anyone* admit **he** was lost?	*Men* should support **themselves**. *Ann and Ed* planned **their** future. Did *both* admit **they** were lost?

Singular pronouns refer to singular antecedents; plural pronouns refer to plural antecedents.

These singular antecedents take singular pronouns: *one, each, either, neither, anyone, someone, everyone, no one, somebody, nobody, everybody, anybody, a person, a man, many a man, another.*

These plural antecedents take plural pronouns: *few, both, several, many,* and *others.*

Note: Informal usage permits the plural *they (their, them)* referring to a singular indefinite antecedent, when the sex is not known or when a singular would be very awkward.

So *someone* called when I was gone? What did *they* say?
Since *everybody* in the room liked ice cream, I bought some for *them.*

EXERCISE 1

Combine each pair of sentences below by using a compound subject or a compound subject complement.

A. Paul had been cordial. So had she.

    She and Paul had been cordial.

B. It was Ann. Or it was they.

    It was they or Ann.

C. Mack didn't wear a tie. He didn't either.

    Neither he nor Mack wore a tie.

1. Her brother will be disappointed. So will she.

2. It was Ralph who called. Or it was she.

3. We will not admit defeat. They won't either.

4. Is that Grover knocking? Or is it he?

5. Harvey forgave you. So did we.

6. Was it Kate who protested? Or was it they?

7. Why did you mention that? Why did he?

8. We didn't have any bananas. They didn't either.

_____

9. Was Dan the winner? Or was she?

_____

10. It was you who did it. Or it was he.

_____

EXERCISE 2

Make word substitutions in the following sentences by (a) changing proper nouns to pronouns, (b) substituting *I* for "the speaker" or *we* for "the speakers," or (c) changing "which of them" to *who* or "whichever of them" to *whoever*.

A. Neither Larry nor Margaret wants to play bingo.

Neither he nor she wants to play bingo.

B. It's the speaker who should have known better.

It's I who should have known better.

C. Which of them do you suppose really knows?

Who do you suppose really knows?

1. Is it Clara who is calling?

_____

2. Apparently it is the speakers who have lost.

_____

3. Let whichever of them volunteered take the lead.

_____

4. Either Walter or the speaker will be chosen.

_____

5. Which of them besides us failed?

_____

6. Must it be George or the speaker?

_____

7. Which of them did you say he is?

_____

8. Which of them do you think will be the next president?

_____

9. It's the speakers who should pay for it.

_____

10. Is that Lucille or Bernard at the door?

_____

EXERCISE 3

Using correct pronouns after the words given in parentheses, change the subjects in the following sentences to objects.

    A. You and I were elected by the group.

        (elected) _____ The group elected you and me. _____

        (voted for) _____ The group voted for you and me. _____

    B. She and Greg will be tutored in chemistry by Jim White.

        (tutor) _____ Jim White will tutor her and Greg in chemistry. _____

        (teach . . . to) _____ Jim White will teach chemistry to her and Greg. _____

1. He and I were recognized by Dr. Thomas.

    (recognized) _____

    (spoke to) _____

2. He and Catherine will be reprimanded by the officials.

    (reprimand) _____

    (talk sternly to) _____

3. She and the pets will be looked after by Bernice.

    (look after) _____

    (take care of) _____

4. My brothers and I are supported by our uncle.

    (supports) _____

    (provides for) _____

5. The girls and I were complimented by Mr. Shafer.

    (complimented) _____

    (extended a compliment to) _____

8. Guess whom Kevin took hunting? _____

_____

9. To whom did you say I should show this? _____

_____

10. Whoever Alvin helped down the steps is the one who robbed him. _____

_____

_____

EXERCISE 5

Using the words in parentheses, change the subordinate clauses below to infinitive phrases, using correct pronouns as subjects and as complements of infinitives.

A. Bill asked that you or she answer the telephone.

(wants . . . to answer) _____Bill wants you or her to answer the telephone._____

B. Dr. Nelson knew who should be called in an emergency.

(to call) _____Dr. Nelson knew whom to call in an emergency._____

1. Mr. Clark requested that you and I lead the discussion.

(wants . . . to lead) _____

2. Don hopes that he may see you and her tonight.

(to see) _____

3. They quarreled about who should be invited.

(to invite) _____

4. The man upstairs asked that you and I turn down the hi-fi.

(to turn) _____

5. Mr. Parker demands that Jones and they cooperate.

(wants . . . to cooperate) _____

6. The captain decided who would be sidelined next Saturday.

(to sideline) _____

7. I suppose that she and Joe will be late for dinner.

(expect . . . to be) _____

8. Kate wondered who should be informed.

(to inform) _____

9. She promised that she would write him and me.

(to write) _____

10. Helen wishes that she could visit him and Mrs. Hayes.

(to visit) _____

EXERCISE 6

Oral drill: Read each of the following correct sentences aloud twice—the first time saying the words inside the parentheses and the second time omitting the words in the parentheses.

1. He told me more than (he told) *her.*

2. He told me more than *she* (did).

3. Mother can entertain him as well as (she can entertain) *me.*

4. Mother can entertain him as well as *I* (can).

5. Are you as happy as *I* (am)?

6. They are even more concerned that *we* (are).

7. He takes more exercise than *she* (does).

8. Did she treat you as courteously as (she treated) *him?*

9. Did she treat you as courteously as *he* (treated you)?

10. We are more optimistic than *they* (are).

EXERCISE 7

Follow the pattern of the examples as you change each pair of sentences below to one sentence. Be sure to use correct pronouns after *than* or *as* and to omit unnecessary words.

A. He washes cars well. I do not wash them that well.

(better than) _____He washes cars better than I._____

B. Ralph holds the baby awkwardly. So does she.

(as awkwardly as) _____Ralph holds the baby as awkwardly as she._____

1. He eats very slowly. I do not eat that slowly.

(more slowly than) _____

2. I play tennis well. He can play just as well.

(as well as) _____

3. She annoys Dick. And she annoys me.

(as well as) _____

4. I drink very little coffee. They drink a great deal of it.

(less coffee than) _____

5. Patsy is old. In comparison, we are very young.

(much older than) _____

6. We were disappointed. They were equally so.

(as disappointed as) _____

7. Father admires Mr. Evans. Father also admires her.

(as well as) _____

8. Father admires Mr. Evans. We do too.

(as well as) _____

9. You surprised Edna. You also surprised me.

(as well as) _____

10. They are powerful. But we are equally powerful.

(as powerful as) _____

EXERCISE 8

Fill in each blank below by using one of the following as an appropriate appositive to the italicized word or words:

you and I	you and me
she or Ann	her or Ann
they and Sam	them and Sam

1. They need *us waterboys*—_____—at the game.

2. Let*'s* _____ go early.

3. *We freshmen*, especially _____, need guidance.

4. They called *us* seasoned *travelers*—_____.

5. Will *we two*, _____, be invited to the dance?

6. Which *girl* will be the winner, _____?

7. The prettiest *girl*, _____, should win.

8. I'll vote for the prettiest *girl*, _____.

9. The mayor will crown *one* of the girls queen, _____.

10. We listened to the good *debaters*, _____.

11. Our *opponents*, _____, won the debate.

12. It is our *opponents*, _____, who will probably win.

13. All of our *friends*, particularly _____, congratulated us.

14. A camp *cook*, _____, will scramble the eggs.

15. Ask the *boys*, _____, about surf riding.

16. It's amazing to see how much *we* have accomplished, _____.

17. It's almost time for the *two* of us, _____, to refuel the engine.

18. The company *lawyers*, _____, will outmaneuver their opponents.

19. Either *girl*, _____, can play the piano.

20. Let's _____ sit in the balcony.

Name _____ Section _____ Date _____

EXERCISE 9

Change each italicized clause below to a gerund phrase introduced by a possessive pronoun.

    A. *That I take the money* was what she wanted.

      <u>My taking the money was what she wanted.</u>

    B. I did not recall *that he had said that.*

      <u>I did not recall his having said that.</u>

1. *That he changed his mind* was unfortunate.

_____

2. I remember *that they quoted Milton.*

_____

3. You understand *that he does not know the difference.*

_____

4. *That I had cut class deliberately* angered my professor.

_____

5. He emphasizes *that it is the only one in existence.*

_____

6. Our sponsor forgot *that we had scheduled a meeting.*

_____

7. *That they passed the finals* surprised everybody.

_____

8. I remember *that he was late for his wedding.*

_____

9. I cannot imagine *that he failed the test.*

_____

10. *That we sang off key* did not faze the director.

_____

EXERCISE 10

Make sure that pronouns agree in number with their italicized antecedents as you fill in the blanks below.

A. *Few* said *they* were tired.   *Each* said <u>he was tired.</u>

B. *Both* wrote *their* dads.   *Others* wrote <u>their dads.</u>

C. *People* have only *themselves*   A *person* has only <u>himself to blame.</u>
to blame.

1. People may not know their own   A *person* may not know _____
minds.   _____

2. Many a man distrusted himself.   Many *men* distrusted _____

3. Neither said he was sorry.   *Jim* and *Al* said _____
                                    _____

4. Many helped themselves.   *Someone* helped _____

5. Both offered their assistance.   *Several* offered _____
                                    assistance.

6. A few took skis with them.   *Neither* took skis with _____

7. Women show their emotions.   A *woman* shows _____

8. Everyone said he had seen that   *Both* said _____
movie.   that movie.

9. Another contributed his ideas.   *Others* contributed _____
                                    ideas.

10. People have their pet theories.   A *person* has _____

11. All did their best.   *No one* did _____

12. Several got their feet wet.   *Nobody* got _____

13. Some were all by themselves.   *Nobody* was all by _____

14. Nobody gave his views.

Everybody gave _____

15. A child can do it for himself.

Children can do it for _____

16. Each said his daily prayer.

Few said _____

17. Both talked about themselves.

Several talked about _____

18. Many did their duty.

Everybody did _____

19. People ask why they fail.

Everyone asks why _____

20. Many carried their books with them.

Neither carried _____

_____

EXERCISE 11

Following the pattern of the examples, fill in the blanks by converting the simple sentences to gerund phrases introduced by a possessive pronoun.

A. You changed the rule. C. They cut the price.
B. He is homesick. D. She forgot the assignment.

A. I understand _your changing the rule._

B. I understand _his being homesick._

C. I understand _their cutting the price._

D. I understand _her forgetting the assignment._

1. You wrapped the packages. 3. She cared for my dad.
2. He wrote regularly. 4. They sent me a gift.

1. I appreciate _____

2. I appreciate _____

3. I appreciate _____

4. I appreciate _____

5. I play the radio often. 8. They are indifferent.
6. You act like a clown. 9. It is too long.
7. We switched sides. 10. He pretends to be wise.

5. Sue disapproves of _____

6. Sue disapproves of _____

7. Sue disapproves of _____

8. Sue disapproves of _____

9. Sue disapproves of _____

10. Sue disapproves of _____

REVIEW EXERCISE A

Following the pattern of the examples, use *who* or *whom* correctly in subordinate clauses.

I admire Helen. She writes entertaining letters.

a. (who)   I admire Helen, <u>who writes entertaining letters.</u>

b. (whom)   Helen, <u>whom I admire,</u> writes entertaining letters.

1. Mrs. O'Hare wrangled with the driver. He threatened a go-slow strike.

a. (who)   Mrs. O'Hare wrangled with the driver, _____

_____

b. (whom)   The driver, _____

_____, threatened a go-slow strike.

2. Thomas More wrote about Richard III. More disliked him.

a. (who)   Thomas More, _____,
disliked him.

b. (whom)   Thomas More wrote about Richard III, _____

_____

3. Jeri mistrusts Milo. He saw him squander a borrowed quarter.

a. (who)   Jeri, _____, saw him
squander a borrowed quarter.

b. (whom)   Jeri distrusts Milo, _____

_____

4. Frank stared at the pretty cashier. She pretended not to know him.

a. (who)   Frank stared at the pretty cashier, _____

_____

b. (whom)   The pretty cashier, _____

_____, pretended not to know him.

5. The drill sergeant berated the four privates. They snapped to attention.

a. (who)   The drill sergeant berated the four privates, _____

_____

b. (whom)   The four privates, _____

_____, snapped to attention.

REVIEW EXERCISE B

Following the pattern of the examples, fill in the blanks with gerund phrases introduced by possessive pronoun forms.

A. Ted was delayed only five minutes in traffic. That small delay caused him to miss his train.

    His being delayed only five minutes in traffic caused Ted to miss his train.

B. Professor Jones was shocked. The freshmen asked for a double period in chemistry lecture.

    Professor Jones was shocked by their asking for a double period in

    chemistry lecture.

1. Miss Vernon objects to even the slightest whispers in the library. This seems unreasonable to me.

    _____

    _____ seems unreasonable to me.

2. My roommates were furious. Ike had set the alarm two hours ahead of time.

    My roommates were furious at _____

    _____

3. Herman dictated in jet-propelled syllables and demanded perfect copy. The new secretary wept.

    Because of _____

    _____, the new secretary wept.

4. I forgot to cancel Mr. Anderson's appointment with the personnel manager. It was a costly mistake.

    _____

    _____ was a costly mistake.

5. The French soldiers trusted her. This gave the Maid of Orleans courage.

   _____ gave the
   Maid of Orleans courage.

6. The janitor brought order to the paper-littered gym. It was a Herculean labor.

   _____

   _____ was a Herculean labor.

7. Kenneth bowls every Saturday night. Lucille strongly disapproves of this.

   Lucille strongly disapproves of _____

   _____

8. We let the record play on. This was a form of sleep teaching.

   _____ was a
   form of sleep teaching.

9. They talked confidently for hours. It did not solve their problems.

   _____ did
   not solve their problems.

10. Mary fluffed the pillows. It was a daily ritual.

    _____ was a
    daily ritual.

REVIEW EXERCISE C

Change each italicized word or word group below to a correct pronoun form, writing each in order in the space provided. (Do not use indefinite pronouns in this exercise.)

A. Between *Sidney* and Linda there are no secrets.   <u>him</u>

B. Was it *Kathy* who seriously considered moving   <u>she</u>

  in with Berta and *her sisters*?   <u>them</u>

1. I oiled my machine sooner than *Raymond.*   _____

2. *Mr. Lake* and his wife invited Mr. and Mrs. Davis   _____

  over just to meet you and *Elizabeth.*   _____

3. *Ernest's* eating so many prunes made Helen and   _____

  her brothers laugh.   _____

4. Adam bragged about Diana and *her father.*   _____

5. My favorite relatives, *Aunt Rieka* and Uncle Ed,   _____

  sauntered past George and *Gertrude.*   _____

6. Did you or *Tom* write an essay on hiccoughing?   _____

7. The essay won a prize for you and *Victor.*   _____

8. The scene-stealers were *Sir Toby* and Maria.   _____

9. He looked as forlorn as Oliver and *other orphans.*   _____

10. *Jack* and the tired scouts straggled into camp.   _____

11. Stella can deep-sea fish as well as *Don.*   _____

12. You and *David* can, I believe, wield batons   _____

  faster than *the seniors.*   _____

13. Nathan can cut hair better than *his father*. _____

14. We clowns, *Charles* and I, burst out laughing. _____

15. Be sure to get in touch with Mason and *Charles*. _____

16. As for William and *Evelyn*, they like their
    steaks well done. _____

using modifiers 4

1

POSITIVE	COMPARATIVE	SUPERLATIVE
Act I was *funny*.	Act II was *funnier*.	Act III was *funniest*.
I feel *bad*.	I have felt *worse*.	I felt *worst* of all.
We played *well*.	They played *better*.	You played *best* of all.
All are *beautiful*.	Which of the two is *more beautiful?*	Which of the three is *most beautiful?*

Use the comparative degree of a modifier when relating two persons or things (or two groups); use the superlative form when comparing three or more persons or things (or groups).

Note: Informal usage has numerous superlatives comparing only two.

Put your *best* foot forward.
Sadie is the *smartest* one of the twins.
I took the *biggest* half.

2

ADJECTIVES	ADVERBS
The *bashful* child ran away.	The child *bashfully* accepted.
It was a *mortal* wound.	He was *mortally* wounded.
As *usual*, you are right.	You are *usually* right.

The *-ly* ending usually changes an adjective to an adverb.

3

ADVERBS AFTER ACTION VERBS	ADJECTIVES AFTER LINKING VERBS
Drive *carefully*.	Be *careful*.
The stagehand paints *badly*.	The stagehand feels *bad*.
It got out of traps *easily*.	It got *easy* after a while.

As a rule, adverbs follow action verbs; adjectives, linking verbs.

Note: Adverbs, of course, may modify any type of verb, and adverbs may precede and modify an adjective subject-complement.

The stagehand *really* feels *unusually* bad.

4

Only Margaret will write notes to Jim. (Only she?)
Margaret will *only* write notes to Jim. (Not mail them?)
Margaret will write *only* notes to Jim. (Not letters?)
Margaret will write notes *only* to Jim. (Not to Bill?)

The placement of single-word modifiers affects meaning.

Note: Single words which modify the rest of the sentence can shift position without affecting meaning.

> *Soon* Margaret will write Jim.
> Margaret will *soon* write Jim.
> Margaret will write Jim *soon*.

5

Playing tennis this morning, I broke the racket.
The cake *baked by Oliver* tastes surprisingly good.
The news analyst continued, his voice *trembling a little.*

Participial phrases are usually next to words they modify.

EXERCISE 1

Give the comparative and superlative forms of each of the following modifiers. If your college dictionary does not list a form change, use *more* and *most*.

POSITIVE	COMPARATIVE	SUPERLATIVE
A. sure	surer	surest
B. quietly	more quietly	most quietly
1. rare		
2. frequent		
3. good		
4. foggy		
5. satisfactory		
6. reasonably		
7. far		
8. contented		
9. bad		
10. attractive		
11. great		
12. free		
13. little		
14. stubborn		
15. carefully		
16. lovely		
17. freely		

18. realistic   _____   _____

19. interesting   _____   _____

20. versatile   _____   _____

EXERCISE 2

Following the pattern of the examples, correctly use both the comparative and superlative forms of each modifier.

A. John feels good.

Ellen _feels better than he._

Patrick _feels best of all._

B. John turned around quickly.

Ellen _turned around more quickly than he._

Patrick _turned around most quickly._

1. John feels bad.

Ellen _____

Patrick _____

2. John drove slowly.

Ellen _____

Patrick _____

3. John sings well.

Ellen _____

Patrick _____

4. John seemed sure.

Ellen _____

Patrick _____

5. John stood tall.

Ellen _____

Patrick _____

6. John speaks little.

   Ellen _____

   Patrick _____

7. John tangos gracefully.

   Ellen _____

   Patrick _____

8. John finished the job quickly.

   Ellen _____

   Patrick _____

9. John teases hard.

   Ellen _____

   Patrick _____

10. John paints badly.

    Ellen _____

    Patrick _____

EXERCISE 3

By adding -*ly*, change each underlined adjective to an adverb. Then, following the patterns, use the adverb in a phrase by converting the noun either to an adjective or to an -*ing* verb form.

A. whole truth   <u>wholly true</u>

B. gentle touch   <u>gently touching</u>

1. real luck   _____

2. idle gossip   _____

3. reasonable demand   _____

4. sure victory   _____

5. profound thought   _____

6. complete agreement   _____

7. necessary severity   _____

8. faithful attendance   _____

9. extreme brilliance   _____

10. ready answer   _____

11. terrible remorse   _____

12. truthful reply   _____

13. awful loneliness   _____

14. bad play   _____

15. jealous regard   _____

16. quiet happiness   _____

17. cordial welcome   _____

18. blissful ignorance _____

19. unexpected popularity _____

20. striking beauty _____

EXERCISE 4

Oral drill: Read the following sentences aloud several times, giving special attention to the correct italicized modifiers.

1. I am *sure* of it.   I *surely* am puzzled.

2. Is that *real?*   That *really* helps.

3. The band sounds *good.*   The band plays *well.*

4. Our meals were not *regular.*   Our meals were served *regularly.*

5. The answer seemed *correct.*   He answered *correctly.*

EXERCISE 5

Using the linking verb given in parentheses, transform each underlined adjective to a subject complement.

A. the <u>sick</u> child (feels)   The child feels sick.

B. the <u>poor</u> travelers (returned)   The travelers returned poor.

1. the <u>good</u> fruit (looked) _____

2. <u>impatient</u> actors (become) _____

3. her <u>green</u> eyes (are) _____

4. the <u>weary</u> porter (gets) _____

5. one <u>undefeated</u> team (remains) _____

6. a <u>pale</u> contestant (grew) _____

7. some <u>unhappy</u> students (appear) _____

8. the <u>contented</u> dog (seems) _____

9. the <u>docile</u> creature (may be) _____

10. the <u>fascinating</u> goals (became) _____

11. that <u>surprising</u> news (was) _____

12. those <u>bitter</u> apricots (tasted) _____

13. his <u>true</u> words (rang) _____

14. some <u>hysterical</u> voices (sounded) _____

15. those <u>stubborn</u> puppies (acted) _____

16. <u>bright</u> lanterns (burned) _____

17. <u>frivolous</u> waitresses (may be) _____

18. that <u>hopeless</u> situation (seemed) _____

19. the <u>happy</u> bridegroom   (looks)   _____

20. the <u>late</u> train   (could be)   _____

EXERCISE 6

Oral drill: Read the following sentences aloud, placing the modifier before each word in the sentence, discovering (a) where it fits sensibly and (b) whether a shift in its position affects the meaning.

1. (surely)   It is a long walk from here to the lake.

2. (sometimes)   Delia goes on a grapefruit diet before a prom.

3. (really)   Many Southern families eat black-eyed peas on New Year's Day for good luck.

4. (not)   Every place at the table must be marked.

5. (never)   I have trouble keeping even small resolutions.

EXERCISE 7

Following the examples, combine the pairs of sentences by converting the first sentence of each group to a participial phrase that sensibly modifies the subject.

A. Our family drove through the snow on Easter. More than twenty cars in the ditch were counted by us.

Driving through the snow on Easter, our family counted more than twenty

cars in the ditch.

B. Paul was taken by surprise. No answer was ready.

Taken by surprise, Paul had no ready answer.

1. My roommate admitted his mistake. Real courage was shown by him.

_____

2. Jackson dreams of teaching pretty girls. His decision, therefore, was to be a ski instructor.

_____

3. Riggles raised a friendly paw. Lucy's nylons were snagged.

_____

4. The Rangerettes camped by a muddy stream. Open house for mosquitoes was held.

_____

_____

5. The complicated plot involved over twelve major characters. Sandra was bewildered.

_____

_____

6. Picknickers hiked through the woods. Poison ivy was avoided by them.

_____

7. Bates waited sullenly at the intersection. A tired thumb was occasionally waggled by him.

_____

_____

8. Lynn resolved to be a detective. His search for a Dr. Watson was begun.

_____

9. Theda was invited to the Snowflake Hop. Her social ambitions were achieved.

_____

_____

10. I was finishing my chemistry report. My breakfast was forgotten.

_____

REVIEW EXERCISE A

Write a sentence correctly using each of the modifiers below with the word in parentheses, as in the example.

reasonable, reasonably   (price)   a. It's a reasonable price. _____

                                    b. It was reasonably priced. _____

1. good, well   (fight)   a. _____

                          b. _____

2. sure, surely   (miss)   a. _____

                           b. _____

3. bad, badly   (answer)   a. _____

                           b. _____

4. real, really   (display)   a. _____

                              b. _____

5. usual, usually   (order)   a. _____

                              b. _____

6. neat, neatly   (dress)   a. _____

                            b. _____

7. possible, possibly   (cure)   a. _____

                                 b. _____

8. odd, oddly   (word)   a. _____

                         b. _____

9. rough, roughly   (handle)   a. _____

                               b. _____

10. cheap, cheaply   (store)   a. _____

b. _____

REVIEW EXERCISE B

Each word or phrase in the first column may modify a word in the sentence in the second column. Find the word that can be sensibly modified and write it in the blank at the right; then indicate by a caret (∧) where you would place the modifier.

A. surely	Peter∧knows his trade.	knows
B. roaring past	I heard the train∧.	train

1. bad	She played bridge.	_____
2. badly	She played bridge.	_____
3. swatting a fly	Joe broke a cup.	_____
4. skimming the surface	Fish flashed in the sun.	_____
5. sure	It was a victory.	_____
6. surely	It was a victory.	_____
7. bored by petty gossip	Sara kept eating mints.	_____
8. emboldened by success	He made a rash decision.	_____
9. real	He is a prankster.	_____
10. really	He is a prankster.	_____
11. blinded by the light	Mike aimed at the rabbit.	_____
12. blinded by the light	Mike hit an abutment.	_____
13. good	He gave impersonations.	_____
14. well	He gave impersonations.	_____
15. paying tribute to virtue	Hypocrites feign goodness.	_____
16. confident of his support	She willingly takes calculated risks.	_____
17. frying trout	My Siamese cat saw me.	_____

18. having nothing   He wants everything.   _____

19. easy   The problem was solved.   _____

20. easily   The problem was solved.   _____

part **II**

STRUCTURES IN ENGLISH

phrases and sentences **1**

PATTERN 1   a participial phrase reduced to an adjective

   A. a student making inquiries   <u>inquiring student</u>

   B. motors run by electricity   <u>electric motors</u>

1. a flirt having no heart   _____

2. events ending in tragedy   _____

3. an inventor showing ingenuity   _____

4. teachers exercising diplomacy   _____

5. action showing no mercy   _____

6. appearance made in person   _____

7. generalities having no meaning   _____

8. principles based on philosophy   _____

9. days filled with monotony   _____

10. words spoken by a prophet   _____

11. comments giving encouragement   _____

12. answer involving a fallacy   _____

13. astronauts showing no fear   _____

14. situation resulting in confusion   _____

15. greetings bringing cheer   _____

16. love lasting for all eternity   _____

17. hillside having no paths   _____

18. horses showing spirit _____

19. retorts packed with sarcasm _____

20. journey fraught with hazard _____

PATTERN 2   a prepositional phrase reduced to a single-word adjective or adverb

A. It's a course without aims.   It's an aimless course. _____

B. Listen with attention.   Listen attentively. _____

1. It's a class without life.   _____

2. Obey with promptness.   _____

3. It was an hour for decision.   _____

4. Write with regularity.   _____

5. Do it without complaining.   _____

6. It's a hairdo with style.   _____

7. Drive with care.   _____

8. It's a book of importance.   _____

9. He's a man of honor.   _____

10. It's a habit of sophomores.   _____

11. Rule with benevolence.   _____

12. It's a road with many curves.   _____

13. Go in peace.   _____

14. It's an animal with horns.   _____

15. Walk with pride.   _____

16. It's a custom in England.   _____

17. Proceed with caution.   _____

18. Treat it with tolerance.   _____

19. It's an occasion for joy.   _____

20. It was a remark of significance.   _____

PATTERN 3   a participial phrase changed to a hyphenated modifier

A. leaves shaped like a heart   heart-shaped leaves

B. remarks made off the cuff   off-the-cuff remarks

1. pecans covered with chocolate _____

2. letter saying thank you _____

3. a blonde having brown eyes _____

4. machines operated by coins _____

5. dialogue having a quick pace _____

6. students polishing the apple _____

7. roses having long stems _____

8. traffic moving one way _____

9. lawns soaked by rain _____

10. a bid naming no trump _____

11. stocks sold over the counter _____

12. animals eating meat _____

13. a musical shown off Broadway _____

14. shrubs growing fast _____

15. heroes having broad shoulders _____

16. styles being out of date _____

17. tomatoes grown at home _____

18. scores breaking the record _____

19. a clerk showing a quick temper _____

20. ambassadors promoting good will _____

PATTERN 4   a prepositional phrase with a plural object transformed into a hyphenated modifier with a singular noun

    A. vacation of two weeks   two-week vacation _____

    B. tools for changing tires   tire-changing tools _____

1. highway with four lanes   _____

2. drivers in back seats   _____

3. hike of ten miles   _____

4. counter for wrapping gifts   _____

5. friendship of eight years   _____

6. motor with eight cylinders   _____

7. equipment for climbing mountains   _____

8. watch with seventeen jewels   _____

9. cigar for five cents   _____

10. work week of six days   _____

11. container for paper cups   _____

12. play with five acts   _____

13. assignment of four pages   _____

14. gadget for peeling onions   _____

15. gossip in small towns   _____

16. system for saving taxes   _____

17. rain of seven inches   _____

18. desk with five drawers   _____

19. building of three stories   _____

20. music for square dances   _____

PATTERN 5 a participial phrase converted to a possessive noun

A. answer received from James   <u>James' answer</u>

B. a break lasting two weeks   <u>a two weeks' break</u>

1. training given to Martha   _____

2. an engagement lasting two months   _____

3. pride flaunted by Coriolanus   _____

4. secretaries hired by senators   _____

5. choices made by a beggar   _____

6. opinions held by everybody   _____

7. a worth totaling five dollars   _____

8. a ball sponsored by firemen   _____

9. discovery made by the Curies   _____

10. lunch period lasting an hour   _____

11. ear muffs worn by Charles   _____

12. assignment given for Thursday   _____

13. diet prescribed for babies   _____

14. votes cast by the people   _____

15. help coming from others   _____

16. aid given by another   _____

17. questions put by the police   _____

18. paper delivered this morning   _____

19. sonnets written by Keats   _____

20. a conversation lasting forty minutes   _____

PATTERN 6 a prepositional phrase converted to a possessive noun

A. life of an elephant   lives of elephants

   a. _an elephant's life_____   b. _elephants' lives_____

B. gift from his son-in-law   gifts from his sons-in-law

   a. _his son-in-law's gift_____   b. _his sons-in-law's gifts_____

C. gaiety of a child   gaiety of children

   a. _a child's gaiety_____   b. _children's gaiety_____

1. call from an applicant   calls from applicants

   a. _____   b. _____

2. duty of the editor-in-chief   duties of editors-in-chief

   a. _____   b. _____

3. inhumanity of man   inhumanity of men

   a. _____   b. _____

4. hospitality of my relative   hospitality of my relatives

   a. _____   b. _____

5. letter from an aunt   letters from aunts

   a. _____   b. _____

6. aims of my sister-in-law   aims of my sisters-in-law

   a. _____   b. _____

7. rights of a worker   rights of workers

   a. _____   b. _____

8. decisions of the coach   decisions of the coaches

   a. _____   b. _____

9. help of the sergeant-at-arms   help of the sergeants-at-arms

   a. _____   b. _____

10. smiles from a friend   smiles from friends

   a. _____   b. _____

11. passport for a traveler   passports for travelers

   a. _____   b. _____

12. silhouette of a woman   silhouettes of women

   a. _____   b. _____

13. knife of a surgeon   knives of surgeons

   a. _____   b. _____

14. the charter of that city   the charters of those cities

   a. _____   b. _____

15. masterpiece of the poet   masterpieces of poets

   a. _____   b. _____

16. stroke of a swimmer   strokes of swimmers

   a. _____   b. _____

17. songs of the wood pewee   songs of wood pewees

   a. _____   b. _____

18. gestures of the clown   gestures of the clowns

   a. _____   b. _____

19. plans of a science major   plans of science majors

   a. _____   b. _____

20. attitudes of a scientist   attitudes of scientists

   a. _____   b. _____

PATTERN 7   an adjective clause reduced to an appositive

A. The yacht, which is a status symbol, helps his ego.

The _yacht, a status symbol,_____ helps his ego.

B. Count on Mr. Leto, who is a man of his word.

Count on _Mr. Leto, a man of his word._____

1. Hank, who is a germ-fearing hypochondriac, wears a mask.

   _____ wears a mask.

2. That student production, which has been the talk of our campus, has attracted several talent scouts.

   That student _____

   _____ has attracted several talent scouts.

3. This volcano, which is a source of terror, is still active.

   This _____ is still active.

4. The chairman praised Cassidy, who is a well-trained Senate page.

   The chairman praised _____

5. That check, which was an obvious forgery, bounced.

   That _____ bounced.

6. His den, which is a small room on the north side, stays cold.

   His _____ stays cold.

7. She cannot afford face surgery, which is an expensive operation.

   She cannot afford face _____

8. Bread crumbs are sold in that park, which is a haven for birds.

   Bread crumbs are sold in that _____

9. Special postage stamps, which are attractive commemoratives, honor dead heroes.

Special postage _____ honor dead heroes.

10. The sister of the protagonist has a little mind, which is a storehouse for trivia.

The sister of the protagonist has a little _____

_____

PATTERN 8   an appositive shifted to precede the subject

A. This organ, a wheezy antique, should be sold at once.

A wheezy antique, this organ should be sold _____ at once.

B. Claudius, a villain with a conscience, tries to pray.

A villain with a conscience, Claudius tries _____ to pray.

1. The boss, a fanatic for change, gave Timothy the go-ahead.

_____ Timothy the go-ahead.

2. William Godwin, an optimistic philosopher, believed in the perfectability of man.

_____

in the perfectability of man.

3. The document, virtually a study in madness, is famous.

_____ famous.

4. Wisconsin, America's dairyland, leads in cheese production.

_____ in cheese production.

5. Rip van Winkle, a henpecked husband, happily escaped from his wife.

_____

from his wife.

6. His home, a veritable shack, did not sell.

_____ did not sell.

7. Paul, a lover of sunshine, spent the winter in Florida.

_____ the winter in Florida.

8. Marner, a lonely weaver, worked all night on the tablecloth.

_____ all night on the tablecloth.

9. Sitting Bull, chief of the Sioux Indians, beat Custer at the Little Big Horn Battle in 1876.

_____

_____ at the Little Big Horn Battle in 1876.

10. John Greenleaf Whittier, a color-blind poet, could not distinguish red from green.

_____

_____ red from green.

PATTERN 9   an infinitive changed to a gerund

A. To accept responsibility is a mark of maturity.

    Accepting responsibility is a mark of maturity.

B. Gene began to question me.

    Gene began questioning me.

1. To travel requires both time and money.

2. The goose started to lay golden eggs.

3. To hold friends is an art worth cultivating.

4. Eve hates to sing ballads.

5. To eat spaghetti gracefully is a challenge.

6. To have love means to give love.

7. Most students like to see their names in print.

8. Dr. Vernon prefers to read Browning's monologues aloud.

9. Julie started to build a fire.

10. To change the temperature in a room can affect the accuracy of a wall clock.

_____

_____

PATTERN 10   an infinitive phrase after "For" transformed into a gerund phrase with a possessive noun or pronoun

    A. For a woman to keep a secret is a first-class miracle.

       A woman's keeping a secret is a first-class miracle. _____

    B. For them to rely on Bill in that situation seemed foolish.

       Their relying on Bill in that situation seemed foolish. _____

1. For Merle to go swimming in April was not very sensible.

   _____

2. For him to feign coyness was absurd.

   _____

3. For the general to accept a bribe is treason.

   _____

4. For Robbie to start kindergarten saddens his mother.

   _____

5. For you to operate that automat takes sense as well as cents.

   _____

6. For a waiter to refuse a tip is unheard of.

   _____

7. For Sally to elope appeared unthinkable.

   _____

8. For them to by-pass London seems strange.

   _____

9. For you to propose to her took courage.

   _____

10. For a man to admit that his wife can drive is rare.

_____

PATTERN 11   an infinitive phrase shifted from the subject-first position to the delayed-subject position after the expletive "It"

> To break the ice is not easy.
>
> It is not easy to break the ice. _____

1. To convince him of that would be difficult.

    _____

2. To forfeit the game should not be necessary.

    _____

3. To prolong his term of office would not be wise.

    _____

4. To explain the misunderstanding would take days.

    _____

5. To go against one's conscience unsettles the mind.

    _____

6. To play bridge with his wife irks him.

    _____

7. To replace those furs would take a small fortune.

    _____

8. To take a stroll in this blizzard would be madness.

    _____

9. To haggle over prices was beneath the Bankstons.

    _____

10. To find flaws in Shakespeare is not difficult.

    _____

PATTERN 12   a noun clause converted to an infinitive phrase

Mr. Evans told me how the work should be started.

Mr. Evans told me how to start the work.

1. Phil showed us how the rhumba should be done.

_____

2. I taught him how a conventional gear should be shifted.

_____

3. Matthew told me when the gift should be returned.

_____

4. The jeweler decided how the gem should be mounted.

_____

5. Thoreau considered where his home should be located.

_____

6. We cannot agree on how the roof should be repaired.

_____

7. Alice decided when rehearsals would be held.

_____

8. The freshmen wondered where good pizza pie could be found.

_____

9. Kathy asked where her mink stole could be stored.

_____

10. Frank Lloyd Wright knew how the theater should be built.

_____

PATTERN 13   a noun clause in the delayed-subject position after the expletive "It" shifted to the subject-first position

It was scandalous that he helped his daughter elope!

That he helped his daughter elope was scandalous! _____

1. It is incredible that such advertising can deceive us all.

   _____

2. It seems absurd that a sixty-year-old should play the ingénue!

   _____

3. It is evident that Ray knows his Chaucer backward and forward.

   _____

4. It is uncertain whether the jet can land safely in this fog.

   _____

5. It was sheer luck that the bus stalled just short of the bridge.

   _____

6. It is surprising that crickets chirp more slowly as temperatures fall.

   _____

   _____

7. It was up to the cantankerous foreman whether or not the employees would have a holiday on Christmas Eve.

   _____

   _____

8. It is a fact that hundreds of atomic bombs release less energy than an ordinary hurricane does.

   _____

   _____

9. It is true that the extermination of the American buffalo was due in large measure to the growth of the American railroad.

_____

_____

_____

10. It was hardly a coincidence that a husband as jealous as he returned when he was least expected.

_____

_____

PATTERN 14   a direct question converted to an indirect question

How were the patients getting along?

I asked _how the patients were getting along._____

1. Who was it?

   I asked _____

2. Why was he lurking there?

   I asked _____

3. Where was she in March?

   I asked _____

4. When is Clark going?

   I wonder _____

5. Whose wallet was it?

   I asked _____

6. Why is he a thief?

   I wonder _____

7. Whose birthday was it?

   I asked _____

8. Where may I sign up?

   I wonder _____

9. How have the dogs been?

   I often ask _____

10. What is that gadget?

   I wonder _____

11. Where is the dictionary?

I wonder _____

12. What time is it?

I wonder _____

13. Is it raining now?

I wonder if _____

14. Could he answer?

I asked if _____

15. How fresh were they?

I asked _____

16. Had they waited long?

I asked if _____

17. Is the door locked?

I wonder if _____

18. Is it time to leave?

I wonder if _____

19. How cold is it?

I wonder _____

20. Where could I start?

I asked _____

PATTERN 15 an indirect question converted first to a direct question and then to an exclamation

I wonder how smart Lawrence is.

a. <u>How smart is Lawrence?</u>

b. <u>How smart Lawrence is!</u>

1. I wonder how fresh these tomatoes are.

a. _____

b. _____

2. I asked what colors they were.

a. _____

b. _____

3. I wonder how hard it's raining now.

a. _____

b. _____

4. I'll ask how long the movie is.

a. _____

b. _____

5. I wonder how you can help the cause.

a. _____

b. _____

6. I wonder how happy those June days were.

a. _____

b. _____

7. I'll ask if it's time to shoot.

   a. _____

   b. _____

8. I wonder what surprises are in store.

   a. _____

   b. _____

9. I wonder what surprises there are.

   a. _____

   b. _____

10. I asked how much time it would take.

   a. _____

   b. _____

PATTERN 16   a direct quotation changed to an indirect quotation

A. Bob often says, "I'll work on my disposition—tomorrow."

Bob often says that _he'll work on his disposition tomorrow._____

B. "Why," he asked, "did the jockey take such risks?"

He asked _why the jockey took such risks._____

1. Leon protested, "I ordered caviar instead of sardines."

Leon protested that _____

2. Briggs asked, "Why doesn't Charles sell that jalopy?"

Briggs asked _____

3. "You mustn't whisper backstage," the director told us.

The director told us that _____

4. I noted, "A single moment turns an old year to a new one."

I noted that _____

5. "Why," asked Bernice, "can't I accept both invitations?"

Bernice asked _____

6. Wilfred asked, "How does a long daily coffee break help?"

Wilfred asked _____

7. "You should be good winners," our coach often says.

Our coach often says that _____

8. The executive asked, "Why must taxes be raised again?"

The executive asked _____

9. Mervyn whines, "Nobody loves me, not even myself."

Mervyn whines that _____

10. "Why," Jerry asked, "does Aunt Nell have to be a kill-joy?"

Jerry asked _____

PATTERN 17 an indirect quotation changed to a direct quotation

    A. Paul asked if he could have a raise.

        Paul asked, <u>"Can I have a raise?"</u>

    B. He says that he will be our guide in the Ozarks.

        He says, <u>"I'll be your guide in the Ozarks."</u>

1. The comedian often asks if there is a doctor in the house.

    The comedian often asks, _____

2. He said that he will spend only one week in Madrid.

    He said, _____

3. The Bronco team shouted that they could beat the Huskers.

    The Bronco team shouted, _____

4. Mr. Davis says that we should use the zip code.

    Mr. Davis says, _____

5. Every morning after breakfast she asks what the temperature is.

    Every morning after breakfast she asks, _____

6. Hal answers that he doesn't care what the temperature is.

    Hal answers, _____

7. The landlord says that he has no extra fuses.

    The landlord says, _____

8. Audrey promised that she would go to New York with me.

    Audrey promised, _____

9. Harvey then asked what George's major is.

    Harvey then asked, _____

10. Sid says he'll paint the car if he can borrow it Sunday.

    Sid says, _____

PATTERN 18   an indirect quotation in one sentence transformed into
a direct quotation in two sentences

She replied that George left early this morning and that he was terribly angry.

"George left early this morning," she replied. "He was terribly angry." _____

1. Jean said that Hank did not eat much salad and that he did not even touch
   the T-bone steak.

   _____

   _____

2. Dot complained that Merle doesn't do his share and yet he wants all the
   credit.

   _____

   _____

3. Mr. Thompson says that Don must pay his bill or otherwise he will be evicted
   by noon tomorrow.

   _____

   _____

4. He said that the yellow berries of the sumac aren't edible and that the
   plants themselves are poisonous.

   _____

   _____

5. Pete yelled that he missed the bus and that he is going to spend the weekend
   with us.

   _____

   _____

PATTERN 19 two simple sentences converted to a complex sentence with a nonrestrictive adjective clause

Portia counseled mercy. She served as lawyer.

Portia, _who served as lawyer,_____ counseled mercy.

Portia, _who counseled mercy,_____ served as lawyer.

1. Rex was grumpy. He had a term paper due.

   Rex _____ was grumpy.

   Rex _____ had a term paper due.

2. Lowell grieved over her death. He wrote "She Came and Went."

   Lowell _____ grieved over her death.

   Lowell _____ wrote "She Came and Went."

3. Helen waited at the stage door. She wanted to see Herman.

   Helen _____ waited at the stage door.

   Helen _____ wanted to see Herman.

4. Bill brags of his courage. He does not even fear her.

   Bill _____ brags of his courage.

   Bill _____ does not even fear her.

5. Plutus is the god of wealth. He is pictured with wings.

   Plutus _____ is the god of wealth.

   Plutus _____ is pictured with wings.

6. Hannah was the heroine. She escaped with ten Indian scalps.

   Hannah _____ was the heroine.

   Hannah _____ escaped with ten Indian scalps.

7. Taylor looked perplexed. He did not understand her smiles.

   Taylor _____ looked perplexed.

   Taylor _____ did not understand her smiles.

PATTERN 20 an introductory adverbial clause condensed to an elliptical clause

> When Herman was corrected once, he did not repeat his error.
>
> <u>When corrected once, Herman</u> _____ did not repeat his error.

1. When Becky is not chewing gum, she feels insecure.

   _____ feels insecure.

2. Even if Phil is drafted, he will propose to Nadyne.

   _____ will propose to Nadyne.

3. When his face is seen once, it is not easily forgotten.

   _____ is not easily forgotten.

4. Even if Vickers is acquitted, he is not guiltless.

   _____ is not guiltless.

5. Though the story is lacking in subtlety, it is hilarious.

   _____ is hilarious.

6. While Tom was preparing his acceptance speech, he little dreamed of defeat.

   _____ little dreamed of defeat.

7. If Lacy is asked to contribute, he will give nothing.

   _____ will give nothing.

8. While the boys were waiting, they complained about the test.

   _____ complained about the test.

9. Even if Fay is undecided now, she will come around in time.

   _____ will come around in time.

10. Whenever Boots is called to the phone, she applies lipstick.

_____ applies lipstick.

PATTERN 21   a subjunctive introduced by "If" or "Even if" changed to a subjunctive not introduced by "If" or "Even if"

A. If I were in charge, I'd do differently.

Were I in charge, _____ I'd do differently.

B. If Ames had been present, he would have spoken up.

Had Ames been present, _____ he would have spoken up.

1. If I were a philosopher, I would clearly define *love* and *like*.

_____ I would clearly define *love* and *like*.

2. If you had told me, I would have met your train.

_____ I would have met your train.

3. If Downs should retire, could he live comfortably?

_____ could he live comfortably?

4. If it were possible to move mountains, I'd start on the Rockies.

_____ I'd start on the Rockies.

5. Even if he be ever so humble, Uriah Heep is a social climber.

_____ Uriah Heep is a social climber.

6. If I were Paul, I'd go pick a wallflower.

_____ I'd go pick a wallflower.

7. If he were you, he'd invest the thousand dollars.

_____ he'd invest the thousand dollars.

8. Even if they had bought a car, they could not keep it up.

_____ they could not keep it up.

9. If he were asked where the Haversian canals are, he'd guess Egypt.

_____ he'd guess Egypt.

10. If I were Queen of the Nile, I'd give you a ride on my barge.

_____ I'd give you a ride on my barge.

PATTERN 22 a parenthetical clause converted to a main clause preceded by a semicolon

Achilles, I've read, was almost invulnerable.

Achilles was _almost invulnerable; that is what I've read._____

1. Lady Godiva's horse, I'm told, bore his burden proudly.

   Lady Godiva's horse _____

   _____

2. *Moby-Dick*, I understand, is filled with symbols.

   Moby-Dick _____

3. Unlike a man, a woman, I believe, loves deeply but rarely.

   Unlike a man, a woman _____

   _____

4. Used for herding reindeer, the Samoyed, I've learned, is hardy.

   Used for herding reindeer, the Samoyed _____

   _____

5. Westerns, I've observed, usually have wholly bad or wholly good men.

   Westerns usually have _____

   _____

6. Clara Murdstone is, I think, a woman of steel.

   Clara Murdstone is _____

7. Your mother is, I fear, dreadfully ill.

   Your mother is _____

8. You cannot win, everyone contends, by resisting authority.

   You cannot win _____

9. She may, I've heard, be a compulsive talker.

   She may _____

10. You will, I hope, stay here.

    You will _____

PATTERN 23 a main clause preceded by a semicolon converted to a nominative absolute preceded by a comma

For two hours we laughed and swam in the breakers; the hot sun left white laughter wrinkles on our tanned faces.

For two hours we laughed and swam in the ___breakers, the hot sun leaving___

___white laughter wrinkles on our tanned faces.___

1. Someday the school calendar may be revised; many students feel the need of longer weekends.

   Someday the school calendar may be _____

   _____

2. Burton failed to reach Dr. Adams; the telephone lines were down as a result of the tornado.

   Burton failed to reach _____

   _____

3. Inch by inch the stubborn rock gave way; the powerful bulldozer nudged it aside.

   Inch by inch the stubborn rock _____

   _____

4. Anthropologists wondered at the devotion of the natives to their chief; his laws were stringent, even cruel.

   Anthropologists wondered at the devotion of the natives to their _____

   _____

   _____

5. The captive audience finally succumbed to Morpheus; the speaker droned on for almost two hours about Greek myths.

   The captive audience finally succumbed to _____

   _____

   _____

PATTERN 24   a nominative absolute converted to a main clause preceded by a colon; a subordinate clause changed to a main clause

His temper being snappy, I can understand why they always try to avoid spats with Frank.

They always try to avoid spats with Frank: his temper is snappy.

1. Our Christmas tree still standing on February 4, I can understand why we are the laughing stock of our block.

2. Taste in books differing widely, I can understand why a tremendous variety of paperbacks is available.

3. His health record having been questioned, we can see why the company turned James down.

4. His poetry having such a wide appeal for British readers, I can see why Longfellow has a place in the Poets' Corner.

5. The boys having started a slim-waist fad, I can understand why the malt shop is losing money nowadays.

Name _____ _Section_ _____ _Date_ _____

PATTERN 25   simple sentence changed to compound sentence with its main clauses joined by an adverbial conjunction

> Paul has studied the Egyptians. He speaks, therefore, of Memphis as a lost city and exclaims "Holy cats!" instead of "Holy cow!"
>
> Paul has studied the _Egyptians; therefore, he speaks_ of Memphis as a lost city and exclaims "Holy cats!" instead of "Holy cow!"

1. The Chinese know how to season dehydrated turtle. They know, moreover, how to cook and serve birds' nests.

   The Chinese know how to season dehydrated _____

   _____ how to cook and serve birds' nests.

2. Nobody doubts the existence of plant-eating animals. Few people, however, know of animal-eating plants.

   Nobody doubts the existence of plant-eating _____

   _____ animal-eating plants.

3. Johnny Appleseed loved trees. He likewise loved animals and was especially kind to them.

   Johnny Appleseed loved _____

   _____ especially kind to them.

4. Every day Percy writes a love note to Laura. His pals therefore teasingly call him Petrarch.

   Every day Percy writes a love note to _____

   _____ him Petrarch.

5. You'll not find Mother Carey's chickens in a farmyard. You might, however, ask a sailor about them.

   You'll not find Mother Carey's chickens in a _____

   _____ a sailor about them.

PATTERN 26   a compound sentence with a parenthetical element and an adverbial conjunction converted to simple sentences

> Tyranny, according to Aristotle, is a great evil; however, unrestricted democracy is even worse.

> According to Aristotle, tyranny is a great evil. Unrestricted democracy,

> however, is even worse.

1. Archimedes, in reality, discovered specific gravity; nevertheless, Newton is sometimes erroneously given credit.

2. An onion skin, of course, is the skin of an onion; however, a goldbeater's skin is a membrane from the intestines of an ox.

3. Hindus, according to Dr. Owens, believe in hungry gods; therefore, religious natives stock household shrines with rice.

4. A possum, feigning death, can put on a good show; however, the puffer globefish is more convincing with its death act.

5. We, like Hamlet, are far too often cruel in an attempt to be kind; moreover, like Claudius, we can smile and smile and still be villains.

PATTERN 27 two simple sentences transformed into a compound sentence having main clauses joined by "nor"

> I do not like peas. I don't like corn either.
>
> <u>I do not like peas, nor do I like corn.</u> _____

1. Faye did not worry. She didn't need to either.

   _____

2. Ike will not write. He won't call either.

   _____

3. I did not ask for a raise. I didn't get one either.

   _____

4. Al cannot build a fire. He can't catch fish either.

   _____

5. Vi does not say yes. She doesn't intend to either.

   _____

6. Herb has no car. He doesn't have any money either.

   _____

7. The cold wave has not hit Texas. It hasn't struck Tulsa either.

   _____

8. I had not finished the mopping. I hadn't done the dishes either.

   _____

9. We do not have any pop. We don't have any popcorn either.

   _____

10. Bud is not handsome. He is not tall and dark either.

   _____

1. Tom called, and Ethel was bored.   (until)

    a. _____

    b. _____

2. I taught the parrot to talk, and I covered its cage.   (when)

    a. _____

    b. _____

3. The boys baited the hooks, and the girls squealed.   (while)

    a. _____

    b. _____

4. Kate brushed the dog, and she fed him.   (as soon as)

    a. _____

    b. _____

5. Hank will clean the garage, and Susan will make fudge.   (if)

    a. _____

    b. _____

6. Delia persists, and he grows cantankerous.   (unless)

    a. _____

    b. _____

7. Joe left the field, and his fans applauded.   (before)

    a. _____

    b. _____

PATTERN 32   a complex sentence converted to a simple sentence by changing the subordinate clause to a main clause and the main clause to a prepositional phrase

> When Otis defended himself, he lied.
>
> Otis defended himself by lying. _____

1. When Circe changed men into swine, she used a potion.

   _____

2. When he opened the door, he pried off the lock.

   _____

3. When Don wrote that poem, he used a Spanish model.

   _____

4. When she thanked the porter, she tipped him.

   _____

5. When he wooed her, he offered gifts.

   _____

6. When she wastes time, she stares at the wall.

   _____

7. When he avoided the accident, he took to the ditch.

   _____

8. When Carl teased Sheryl, he kept her waiting.

   _____

9. When he saved the old man's life, he lost his own.

   _____

10. When Hal bought that property, he worked through an agent.

   _____

PATTERN 33 a complex sentence converted to a simple sentence by changing the noun clause to basic sentence parts—with a colon and a series and a parenthetical phrase

> Spinoza believed that avarice and ambition and lust are species of madness.
>
> According to Spinoza, these are species of madness: avarice, ambition, and lust.

1. Duke wrote that poetry and criticism and narration were fields for Poe's genius.

2. Mrs. Dee believes that color TV and electric toothbrushes and king-size cigarettes are symbols of the twentieth century.

3. Philosophers say that death and taxes and love cannot be avoided.

4. Brown maintains that cooking and sewing and baby care should be required courses for every college boy.

5. Clark insists that a car and a tuxedo and a full wallet are the marks of a gentleman.

PATTERN 34 a complex sentence converted to a simple sentence by dropping the expletive and changing the subordinate clause to basic sentence parts

   A. It was in 1945 that World War II ended.

     In 1945 World War II ended. _____

   B. There are three planks that are warped.

     Three planks are warped. _____

1. It was after the third C that he dropped the course.

    _____

2. There are not many men who avoid doing the honorable thing.

    _____

3. It was in 1926 that Gene Tunney won the championship.

    _____

4. There are many success stories which smack of the picaresque.

    _____

5. It was before the wedding that she dyed her hair.

    _____

6. There was Salk, who gave the world polio vaccine.

    _____

7. It was in Ohio that I lost my heart.

    _____

8. It was in May that she flew to Paris.

    _____

9. There is one ad that offers lessons in chess.

_____

10. It was about midnight when the guests had indigestion.

_____

PATTERN 35   a compound sentence converted to a shorter sentence by using a dash and omitting words

Dora always tells the truth; at least, she tells parts of it.

Dora always tells the _truth—parts of it._____ _____

1. Jan admired her teeth; in fact, he admired both of them.

   Jan admired her _____

2. Do it the right way; of course, the right way is my way.

   Do it the right _____

3. You can speak your mind; that is, you can if you whisper.

   You can speak your _____

4. In 1965 Rudolph married; in fact, he married three times.

   In 1965 Rudolph _____

5. She is the girl of his dreams; at least, she is the star of his nightmares.

   She is the girl of his _____

6. Hal likes cats in a way; to be sure, he likes them far away.

   Hal likes cats in _____

7. Only one face ever impressed him; of course, it was the one he saw in the mirror.

   Only one face ever impressed _____

8. She broadcast his virtues; of course, she did so only when no one was tuned in.

   She broadcast his _____

9. There's a place for that poem; in fact, it belongs in the fire.

   There's a place for that _____

10. He is a terrific coach; that is, he coaches well in his armchair.

He is a terrific _____

PATTERN 36   a compound sentence transformed into simple sentences with parentheses and dashes

   A. Greg did not long for change, nor did he fear it.

   Greg did not _long for (or fear) change._____

   Greg did not _long for—or fear—change._____

   B. It is not a hush-hush event, nor is it a hurly-burly one.

   It is not _a hush-hush (or a hurly-burly) event._____

   It is not _a hush-hush—or a hurly-burly—event._____

1. His editorial did not alarm us, nor did it entertain us.

   His editorial did not _____

   His editorial did not _____

2. He is not an unduly meticulous person, nor is he a wantonly careless one.

   He is not _____

   He is not _____

3. Mrs. Wyert does not pamper the child, nor does she abuse him.

   Mrs. Wyert does not _____

   Mrs. Wyert does not _____

4. He is not a prig at a dance, nor is he a fop there.

   He is not _____

   He is not _____

5. I did not criticize his stand, nor did I condone it.

   I did not _____

   I did not _____

6. Doris is not a blasé tourist, nor is she a naïve one.

   Doris is not _____

   Doris is not _____

7. The professor did not wheedle us, nor did he coax us.

   The professor did not _____

   The professor did not _____

8. It was not a Maltese cross, nor was it a Celtic one.

   It was not _____

   It was not _____

9. Frank did not accept my suggestion, nor did he reject it.

   Frank did not _____

   Frank did not _____

10. This is not an Indian gift, nor is it a Greek one.

   This is not _____

   It is not _____

PATTERN 37   two sentences with different end punctuation converted to one sentence with an interrupter set off by dashes

A. Put your best foot forward. Why not your *better?*

  Put your _best—why not your better?—foot forward._

B. Millie thinks toads sit on toadstools. How dumb she is!

  Millie _thinks—how dumb she is!—toads sit on toadstools._

1. Ted pooh-poohed her every suggestion. Isn't that typical?

   Ted _____

2. In the alley Trixie browses among tin cans. As you well know!

   In the alley Trixie _____

3. Johann Strauss could compose a waltz in one morning. Isn't it amazing?

   Johann _____

4. Pete's spelling will fascinate you. He writes *center* for *centaur!*

   Pete's _____

5. Charles has another parking ticket. What luck!

   Charles _____

6. Our happy moments are as short-lived as snowflakes striking a warm windshield. Don't you agree?

   Our happy _____

   _____

7. She thinks even his cowlick is cute. How she loves him!

   She thinks _____

8. Bert absorbed the disappointment remarkably well. Or did he merely resign himself to the inevitable?

Bert _____

_____

9. Her answers amazed the whole class. What a memory!

Her _____

10. The brakes are not working. Heaven help us!

The _____

PATTERN 38 two simple sentences converted to one sentence by omitting words and by using a series and a dash

> In the Southwest there are cactuses, cow ponds, and dust devils. In fact, these things spell the Southwest.

> Cactuses, cow ponds, dust devils—these spell the Southwest.

1. In Ireland there are shamrocks, thatched cottages, dry wit, and blarney. In fact, these things remind me of Ireland.

_____

_____

2. With summer picnics there are busy flies, envious bees, and curious cows. In fact, all these plague summer picnickers.

_____

3. During cram sessions there are gnawed pencils, burnt-out bulbs, and half-empty coffee cups. In fact, these things suggest cram sessions to me.

_____

_____

4. In Shakespeare's comedies there are disguises, mistaken identities, and a "Jill for every Jack." In fact, these are elements in Shakespeare's comedies.

_____

_____

5. In the average glove compartment there are road maps, key rings, Kleenex containers, and empty cigarette packages. In fact, these things stuff the average glove compartment.

_____

_____

6. At homecoming there are the pep rallies, the bonfire, the parade, and the football game. In fact, these activities make homecoming exciting.

   _____

   _____

7. In the Victorian age there were the literary giants Robert Browning, Matthew Arnold, and Alfred, Lord Tennyson. In fact, these men dominated the period.

   _____

   _____

PATTERN 39 a subject-first sentence with an interrupter set off by dashes converted to a sentence with a prepositional phrase first and a parenthetical element last

    A. All of them—Ray and Alec were beside each other—huddled near the fifty-yard line.

    Near the <u>fifty-yard line they all huddled, Ray beside Alec.</u>

    B. The clouds were dark—as dark as a black sea—beneath the plane.

    Beneath the <u>plane the clouds were dark, as dark as a black sea.</u>

1. All of them—Ann and Jane were near each other—sat boohooing in the back row.

    In the _____

    _____

2. My mind was blank—as blank as my stares at the professor—all during the test.

    All during the _____

    _____

3. Several of them—Walter and Bud sat beside each other—shared sundaes at the corner drugstore.

    At the _____

    _____

4. Alma is incurious—as incurious as a Confederate's horse on the courthouse lawn—about European events.

    About _____

    _____

5. Many of them—mothers and their children were with each other—waited impatiently outside the audition room.

    Outside the _____

    _____

5. The Iowa farm boy had dinner with the Georgia belle. He enjoyed her fried chicken. And he complimented her small, heavy biscuits.

The Iowa farm boy had dinner with the Georgia _____

_____

_____

6. She was a happy person. She appreciated the joys of the moment. And she refused to anticipate the gloom of tomorrow.

She was a happy _____

_____

7. He had a formal meeting with Mr. and Mrs. Graham. He requested their daughter's hand. And he secretly wished for their refusal.

He had a formal meeting with Mr. and Mrs. _____

_____

_____

8. The hypochondriac browsed among the medicines. He picked out vitamins and wonder drugs. And he read the fine print of the directions.

The hypochondriac browsed among the _____

_____

_____

9. Frank stepped on the brakes. He turned on the fog lights. And he honked several times.

Frank stepped on the _____

_____

10. She worried him back to health. She prepared nutritious but untasty food. And she woke him every four hours to give him sleeping pills.

She worried him _____

_____

_____

PATTERN 41   three questions converted to one statement with parallel items in a series

> Isn't it true that she wears no make-up? Doesn't she visit any hairdresser? And how about h wearing shoes?

> She uses no make-up, _visits no hairdresser, and wears no shoes._ _____

1. Isn't it true that the comedian wears a wig? Doesn't he flash gold teeth? And how about his sporting pince-nez?

   The comedian wears a wig, _____

   _____

2. Isn't it true that Hines was born in England? Wasn't he educated in Mexico? And how about his being mar ied in Italy?

   Hines was born in England, _____

   _____

3. Isn't it true that Hank went to the Shrimp Boat? Didn't he order the house specialty? And how about his learning to crack lobster claws?

   Hank went to the Shrimp Boat, _____

   _____

4. Isn't it true that the mouse scooted across the hall? Didn't he steal the cheese? And how about his jumping clear of the trap?

   The mouse scooted across the hall, _____

   _____

5. Isn't it true that Joe hated sports? Didn't he avoid gym classes? And how about his refusing even to go to games?

   Joe hated sports, _____

   _____

6. Isn't it true that Vernon raced over to the sideline? Didn't he fake a pass to Hawkes? And how about his dropping the ball on the five-yard line?

Vernon raced over to the sideline, _____

_____

7. Isn't it true that Dora burned the roast? Didn't she use too much rice? And how about her spilling the beans?

Dora burned the roast, _____

_____

8. Isn't it true that we say *put on* instead of *pretend*? Don't we use *put out* rather than *exasperated*? And how about our substituting *put up* for *preserve*?

We say *put on* instead of *pretend*, _____

_____

9. Isn't it true that a twelfth-century merchant valued pins highly? Didn't he pay dearly for a pin? And how about his selling pins legally on only two days of the year?

A twelfth-century merchant valued pins highly, _____

_____

_____

10. Isn't it true that the mother of Achilles dipped him in fire at night? Didn't she rub him with ambrosia by day? And how about her dunking him in the River Styx?

The mother of Achilles dipped him in fire at night, _____

_____

PATTERN 42   three sentences converted to one sentence containing a series of participial phrases and then to another sentence containing a series of infinitive phrases

He lounged in the smoking car. He grumbled about taxes. And he blamed his congressman.

a. I noticed him <u>lounging in the smoking car, grumbling about taxes, and</u>

   <u>blaming his congressman.</u>

b. I expected him <u>to lounge in the smoking car, to grumble about taxes,</u>

   <u>and to blame his congressman.</u>

1. Fred extolled Hemingway's novel. He defended its skimpy characterization. And he praised its terse style.

   a. I heard Fred _____

   _____

   b. I expected Fred _____

   _____

2. The car ahead careened round the sharp curve. It crashed through the safety posts. And it rolled into the creek.

   a. We saw the car ahead _____

   _____

   b. I half expected the car ahead _____

   _____

3. Marvin smiled at the stewardess. He asked for a newspaper. And he pretended to study the stock market report.

   a. We watched Marvin _____

   _____

b. We dared Marvin _____

_____

4. Albert stumbled into the dark laboratory. He knocked over a rack of test tubes. And he made excuses for his behavior.

a. I heard Albert _____

_____

b. I expected Albert _____

_____

5. The man pretended to help her over the ice. He grasped her arm firmly. And he stole her purse and ran away.

a. I saw the man _____

_____

b. I hardly expected the man _____

_____

6. He searched for the extra car keys. He took them out of the desk drawer. And he hid them behind Dad's picture.

a. I watched him _____

_____

b. I told him _____

_____

7. Henry strutted across the stage. He hummed "Show Me the Way To Go Home." And he looked in blank dismay at the laughing audience.

a. We observed Henry _____

_____

b. We dared Henry _____

_____

PATTERN 43 two sentences converted to one sentence by using various parallel structures with "not only . . . but also"

Franklin organized the first lending library. He formed the first volunteer fire department.

a. Franklin organized not only _the first lending library but also the first_ _volunteer fire department._

b. Franklin not only _organized the first lending library but also formed the_ _first volunteer fire department._

c. Not only did Franklin organize _the first lending library, but he also formed_ _the first volunteer fire department._

1. Walt Whitman loved his fellow man. He regarded Abraham Lincoln with special affection.

a. Walt Whitman loved not only _____

_____

b. Walt Whitman not only _____

_____

c. Not only did Walt Whitman love _____

_____

2. After their quarrel, Mildred ignored Bruce. She avoided his friends.

a. After their quarrel, Mildred ignored not only _____

_____

b. After their quarrel, Mildred not only _____

_____

c. After their quarrel, not only did Mildred ignore _____

_____

3. The Ace Manufacturing Company mailed thousands of leaflets. It sent free samples of its product.

   a. The Ace Manufacturing Company mailed not only _____

   _____

   b. The Ace Manufacturing Company not only _____

   _____

   c. Not only did the Ace Manufacturing Company mail _____

   _____

4. Sibyl worries about homeless children. She frets about abused or abandoned dogs.

   a. Sibyl worries not only _____

   _____

   b. Sibyl not only _____

   _____

   c. Not only does Sibyl worry about _____

   _____

5. Cedric knows about the postal system. He understands the dead-letter office.

   a. Cedric knows not only _____

   _____

   b. Cedric not only _____

   _____

   c. Not only does Cedric know about _____

   _____

PATTERN 44 two sentences converted to one sentence with the verb preceding the subject

    A. There is the president of the student council. He has a big say-so.

       Having _a big say-so is the president of the student council._

    B. Mike owns a chinchilla farm. It is about ten miles west of here.

       About _ten miles west of here is Mike's chinchilla farm._

1. There is the new library. It adjoins the historical museum.

   Adjoining _____

2. Taylor has six students. They are among the best debaters in the state.

   Among _____

3. There is an excellent day camp. It overlooks Lake Retna.

   Overlooking _____

4. Jim has a miniature TV. It is in the bathroom.

   In _____

5. There sleeps the indifferent groom. He sits tall in the front pew.

   Sitting _____

6. Coleridge described water snakes. They swam beyond the shadow of the ship.

   Beyond _____

7. There was the dismal parade. It approached us like an unsuccessful door-to-door salesman.

   Approaching _____

   _____

8. Danita has three toy poodles. They are among the finest in the show.

Among _____

_____

9. There was a special-delivery letter. It lay unopened on his desk for days.

Lying _____

_____

10. The child has an Amazonian mother. She was standing near the entrance of the classroom.

Standing _____

_____

PATTERN 45   a loose sentence converted to a periodic sentence by shifting the parenthetical matter to the beginning and by placing a verb or a complement at the end

    A. Misfortunes occur only when a man is false to his own genius, according to Thoreau.

      According to ___Thoreau, only when a man is false to his own genius do___

      misfortunes _____ occur.

    B. An educated person tells no lies because of his resourcefulness, generally speaking.

      Generally ___speaking, because of his resourcefulness an educated person tells___

      no _____ lies.

1. Salt or hesitation is good only when it is used in little measure, according to the Talmud.

    According to _____

    _____ good.

2. Chanticleer's fears vanish as soon as daylight arrives, in Chaucer's mock epic.

    In _____

    _____ vanish.

3. Her tongue started wagging not five minutes after she had threatened never to speak to him again, strangely enough.

    Strangely _____

    _____

    _____ wagging.

4. A man willingly receives charity only when it is love instead of a handout, in my opinion.

    In _____

    _____ charity.

5. Brutus agreed to join the conspiracy only out of concern for Rome, if we are to believe Shakespeare.

   If _____

   _____ conspiracy.

6. Jumeau originated an extraordinary fashion doll in order to outdo German markets, as has been noted.

   As _____

   _____ fashion doll.

7. Ernest offers to wash the dishes only when his wife uses paper plates, if the rumor is true.

   If _____

   _____ dishes.

8. Bevo has few really close friends because of his egg and onion diet, as anyone can readily understand.

   As anyone _____

   _____ friends.

9. Ruth compliments us only when she wants a favor, as a matter of fact.

   As a _____

   _____ us.

10. Fra Lippo Lippi exclaims "Zooks!" both at the beginning and at the end of his monologue, quite in character.

   Quite _____

   _____

   _____ "Zooks!"

PATTERN 46   a compound sentence condensed by substituting a comma for words already stated

> The father of that large family wants to buy a station wagon; the mother wants to buy a fourteen-passenger bus.
>
> The father of that large family wants to buy a station <u>wagon; the mother, a</u>
>
> <u>fourteen-passenger bus.</u>

1. According to some ancients, a small dose of mandrake made a man proud; a large dose of mandrake made a man insane.

   According to some ancients, a small dose of mandrake made a man _____

   _____

2. Success may be best understood by a failure; defeat may be best understood by a winner.

   Success may be best understood by a _____

   _____

3. In Canada, November 11 is called Remembrance Day; in the United States, November 11 is called Veterans' Day.

   In Canada, November 11 is called Remembrance _____

   _____

4. Washington Irving chose Geoffrey as a penname; Benjamin Franklin chose Richard.

   Washington Irving chose Geoffrey as a _____

   _____

5. In the sixteenth century a competitor was a partner; in the early twentieth century a competitor was a rival.

   In the sixteenth century a competitor was a _____

   _____

6. When a boy is five, he brings his sweetheart dandelions; when he is fifteen, he brings her orchids.

   When a boy is five, he brings his sweetheart _____

   _____   _____

7. To Robert Burns' young lover the Rye was a river; to Salinger's Holden the Rye was a field.

   To Robert Burns' young lover the Rye was a _____

   _____

8. Jeannie dreams of receiving an Academy Award; her sister dreams of receiving an Emmy.

   Jeannie dreams of receiving an Academy _____

   _____

9. To the sailor a red sky in the morning means trouble; a red sky at night means sailors' delight.

   To the sailor a red sky in the morning means _____

   _____

10. "A smilet is correctly defined as a little smile," Jude facetiously remarked; "a hamlet is correctly defined as a little ham."

   "A smilet is correctly defined as a little smile," Jude facetiously _____

   _____

PATTERN 47 a compound sentence converted to a complex sentence using "so . . . that" instead of a transitional expression and using an active instead of a passive verb

> The pudding was scorched and lumpy; in fact, it was called a burnt offering by the cook.
>
> The pudding was <u>so scorched and lumpy that the cook called it a burnt</u>
>
> <u>offering.</u>

1. His remarks were delightfully clever; as a result, even his enemies were amused by them.

   His remarks were _____

   _____

2. The test questions were difficult; as a matter of fact, even the brightest students were stymied by them.

   The test questions were _____

   _____

3. The lover's vision is transcendent; as a result, wonderful beauties are seen in his beloved and in himself by the lover.

   The lover's vision is _____

   _____

4. The solution is flammable; in fact, a fire can be started by a spark from a cigarette.

   The solution is _____

   _____

5. His arguments are peppery; in fact, they ought to be sneezed at by any thinking person.

   His arguments are _____

   _____

6. Traffic on the toll bridge was snarled; therefore, the helicopter passengers above were envied by frustrated motorists.

Traffic on the toll bridge was _____

_____

7. An ex-wrestler, the dentist was clumsy; in fact, his patient's jaws were bruised by him.

An ex-wrestler, the dentist was _____

_____

8. The smog was thick; as a result, the cub plane could not be landed by James.

The smog was _____

_____

9. Being with her was pleasant; as a matter of fact, he was bored by the company of anyone else.

Being with her was _____

_____

10. The professor is scholarly; as a result, little of his lectures can be understood by us freshmen.

The professor is _____

_____

PATTERN 48 a subject-first sentence changed to begin with a prepositional phrase (with an object of a verb changed to an object of a preposition) and to end with a noun (converted from a principal verb) following *provides*.

> The idea of fame for himself or glory for his school does not inspire the athlete too indifferent to observe training rules.
>
> For _the athlete too indifferent to observe training rules, the idea of fame for_
>
> _himself or glory for his school provides no inspiration._

1. A hasty criticism or an untimely laugh does not encourage the beginning speech student too timid to try again.

    For _____

    _____

2. A curve sign on a freeway or toll road does not help the man too sleepy to see.

    For _____

    _____

3. The desolation of blackened forests or debris-covered fields does not warn the motorist too careless to put out a glowing match.

    For _____

    _____

    _____

4. The phrase "excellent fishing facilities" on advertising leaflets or vacation folders does not allure the executive too busy to relax.

    For _____

    _____

    _____

5. A call to help the poor or to assist the sick does not challenge the family too selfish to share good fortune.

For _____

_____

_____

6. Pieces of sticks or twine will serve to support the plants too weak to climb unaided.

For _____

_____

7. The joy of inquiry or of discovery does not excite the freshman too indolent to study.

For _____

_____

PATTERN 49   a simple sentence changed to a compound–complex sentence by transforming the noun phrase into a noun clause, with inverted word order, and by repeating the verb (with its object)

A. Nobody really knew Frank's beliefs, not even Frank himself.

What <u>Frank believed nobody knew; not even Frank himself knew it.</u>

B. Everybody likes Sally's cooking, even Sally herself.

What <u>Sally cooks everybody likes; even Sally herself likes it.</u>

1. Nobody understood the major's decision, not even the major himself.

   What _____

   _____

2. Everybody ignores Tony's advice, even Tony himself.

   What _____

   _____

3. Nobody heard the general's order, not even the general himself.

   What _____

   _____

4. Everybody enjoyed Wanda's quoting, even Wanda herself.

   What _____

   _____

5. Nobody remembers Otis' contributions, not even Otis himself.

   What _____

   _____

6. Everybody praised his writing, even the author himself.

   What _____

   _____

7. Everybody questioned the poet's meaning, even the poet himself.

   What _____

   _____

8. Everybody admires the boss's plans, even the boss himself.

   What _____

   _____

9. Nobody knows that Texan's dream, not even the Texan himself.

   What _____

   _____

10. Nobody believed the child's imaginings, not even the child himself.

    What _____

    _____

REVIEW EXERCISE

From the items given, form a sentence patterned on the model. Hold strictly to the word order of the model and give careful attention to form changes (tense, number, case) and punctuation. Occasionally you will have to change one part of speech to another: *energy—energetic.*

Model: Our going to the out-of-the-way place to embark in the restaurant business was mother's idea. —SHERWOOD ANDERSON

they / fly / to the / south of the border / school / to participate / in the government experiment / be / Dad / brainstorm

Their flying to the south-of-the-border school to participate in the

government experiment was Dad's brainstorm.

1. I / climb / on the / stay off the grass / sign / to peer / into the picture window / be / Neal / suggestion

_____

_____

Model: Dwan laughed, but the women didn't. —RING LARDNER

2. service / improve / but / the meal / do not

_____

3. Louise / jump / but / the fireman / cannot

_____

Model: The wagon wheels banged and clattered on the frozen ground; the sky was fixed and brilliant. —WILLIAM FAULKNER

4. the wild stallion / wheel / and / crash / through the lock gate / the moon / be / dim / and / sullen

_____

_____

Model: "Polyphemus," said Mrs. Charles in her oddly unchildish voice, "have you any illusions?" Polyphemus lashed his tail. —ELIZABETH BOWEN

5. Squibbs / coax / Mr Latimer / in / he / curious / boy / way / have / you / any comment / Squibbs / open / he / beak

_____

_____

Model: Enemy-occupied territory—that's what this world is. —C. S. LEWIS

6. parent / patrol / area / that / be / what / I / home / be

_____

7. television / addict / clan / that / be / what / he / family / be

_____

Model: His white mustache, ragged and yellowing at the fringes, drooped in a melancholy wave. —ALDOUS HUXLEY

8. he / lanky hand / callous / and / stiffen / from the chore / reach / for the rusty hoe

_____

_____

Model: A big, burly, choleric dog, he always acted as if he thought I wasn't one of the family. —JAMES THURBER

9. a small / homely / energy / delinquent / he / always behave / as if / he / believe / I / be not / one of the jury

_____

_____

Model: When Mrs. Bates came down, the room was strangely empty, with a tension of expectancy. —D. H. LAWRENCE

10. when / Mr Carter / look up / the sky / be / curious / melancholy / with a promise of snow

_____

_____

11. after / Dr Hayes / drop in / the patient / become / mysterious / quiet / with an air of resignation

_____

_____

Model: Of the three matadors one was ill and trying to conceal it; one had passed his short vogue as a novelty; and the third was a coward. —ERNEST HEMINGWAY

12. of the three / actor / one / appear / humble / and / will / to prove it / one / enjoy / he / brief reign / as a star / and / the third / be / a barnstormer

_____

_____

_____

Model: It was a ladylike yawn, a closed-mouth yawn, but you couldn't miss it; her nostril wings gave her away. —J. D. SALINGER

13. it / be / a synthetic smile / a purse lip / smile / but / you / cannot mistake it / she / cold eye / show / she / up

_____

_____

_____

Model: He had no interests, apparently, but his baking and his hatred, though now that I am older I begin to see other sides to his nature—it did contain, perhaps, a certain furtive love. —GRAHAM GREENE

14. he / have / no fault / particular / except / he / heckle / and / he / pride / although now that / I / be / wise / I / begin / to recognize / other facet / of / he / character / it / show / occasional / a definite hangdog humility

_____

_____

_____

paragraphs 2

PARAGRAPH 1

Today, as in the past, opinions on the bath are anything but unanimous. Some learned doctor proved to his great satisfaction—I do not remember by what stratagem—that man can live a long life in perfect health without ever taking a bath or, for that matter, without washing himself, and at one time or other everybody comes across a person who is living proof of the doctor's theory. Among us the belief in the wholesomeness of bathing is of very recent date and, what with the shakiness of most of our beliefs, bathing might very well fall into oblivion should somebody come up with a more attractive, though not necessarily better, idea. —BERNARD RUDOFSKY[1]

ASSIGNMENT 1

Using Paragraph 1 as your model, write about 100 words giving an interesting, original treatment to a commonplace event, custom, or notion.

TIPS
1. State your main idea clearly and concisely in the first sentence of your paragraph.
2. Develop this controlling idea by presenting unusual details.
3. Make sure that every sentence in your paragraph is related to the topic.

SUGGESTED TOPICS
the futility of haircuts (sleeping), advantages of taking tests (being poor), useless decorations (cosmetics, social customs)

PARAGRAPH 2

One of these friends was Rip, who was a sort of soft character. I guess he was a big liver-and-white springer spaniel, but I don't believe he was much of a looker or a hunter either. Rip had droopy yellow eyes and a mighty mournful expression; he was known around our place as "Old Tear in Me Eye." However poor in the field or worthless he may have been, he did have one outstanding talent, which was catching flies. In summer he sat morosely out on a big rock in the sun and just snapped them up like a skunk eating bees. His precision was unerring, and I watched him with spellbound admiration. —ELIZABETH R. CHOATE[2]

---

[1] From *The Kimono Mind*, by Bernard Rudofsky, pp. 134–35. Copyright © 1965 by Bernard Rudofsky. Reprinted by permission of Doubleday & Company, Inc.

[2] From Elizabeth R. Choate, "Give Your Heart to a Dog," *The Atlantic Monthly* (December, 1964), p. 52. Copyright © 1964 by The Atlantic Monthly Company, Boston, Mass. Reprinted by permission of the author.

ASSIGNMENT 2

Using Paragraph 2 as your model, write a descriptive paragraph of about a hundred words.

TIPS

1. First, name the person or thing to be described and single out one characteristic to be explained.
2. After giving vivid descriptive details, show the person or thing in action.
3. End the paragraph by giving your attitude toward that characteristic action.

SUGGESTED TOPICS

a jalopy that is temperamental, a friend who makes an art of saying *no*, a *now*-how-are-you-going-to-entertain-me guest

PARAGRAPH 3

Supper was excitement. The heavy bowls of sugar and the pitchers of syrup shook with the vibration of the straining engines. There were heavy platters of thick-sliced country ham with red gravy, and of fried, tough round steak. There were bowls of stewed corn, string beans, boiled potatoes, and huge plates of soda biscuits and square-cut pieces of cornbread. There were always fresh round "pounds" of butter, soon gashed and reduced by the reaching knives. Strong coffee was poured from graniteware coffee pots into heavy, handleless cups. And always everything shook with the laboring of the wide paddle wheel as the heavy-loaded boat moved upstream.   —RALPH MC GILL[3]

ASSIGNMENT 3

Write a paragraph of about 100 words developing the topic sentence by listing explanatory items as in the model above.

TIP

Make sure that each item in the list directly relates to the key words (such as *supper* and *excitement* in Paragraph 3) in your topic sentence.

SUGGESTED TOPIC SENTENCES

These borrowed things I intend to return.
The evening was full of surprises.
I have an assortment of favorite sayings.

PARAGRAPH 4

I've never been able to whistle at girls. When an attractive girl went by, I could never muster a long, low whistle. No, I had to put it into words, something

---

[3] From *The South and the Southerner*, by Ralph McGill. Copyright © 1959, 1963 by Ralph McGill. Reprinted by permission of Atlantic–Little, Brown and Company, publishers.

like: "Welllllllll, now!" I never meant it disrespectfully, but it always sounded that way. If I wanted the young lady to know I appreciated her, I had to get up close where she could see me and show my appreciation with facial expressions. That led to all sorts of misunderstandings, including one marriage. *And* one marriage, I guess I should say. —RALPH REPPERT[4]

ASSIGNMENT 4

Using Paragraph 4 as a model, write an informal paragraph of about 100 words.

TIPS

1. Write a short first sentence, selecting one of the suggested topic sentences below or composing one of your own.
2. Use the first-person point of view consistently.
3. Imitate both the simplicity and the conciseness of the model.

SUGGESTED TOPIC SENTENCES

I've never been able to remember names—or faces.
I can't understand football (Shakespeare, the slide rule).
I have at least one fault (such as absent-mindedness).

PARAGRAPH 5

Virginia Woolf had a moonlit transparent beauty. She was exquisitely carved, with large thoughtful eyes that held no foreshadowing of that tragic end which was a grief to everyone who had ever known her. To be in her company was delightful. She enjoyed each butterfly aspect of the world and of the moment, and would chase the lovely creatures, but without damaging the colored dust on their wings. Whenever anyone present said anything pregnant, she would clasp her long delicate hands together and laugh with pleasure. In her own talk she always went straight to the point. For instance, on the first occasion when I met her, at a dinner party given by Osbert and Sacheverell, she asked me, "Why do you live where you do?" "Because I have not much money." "How much money a year have you?" I told her. "Oh well, I think we can do better for you than that," she said thoughtfully. —EDITH SITWELL[5]

ASSIGNMENT 5

Using Paragraph 5 as a model, write a character sketch of about 150 words.

TIPS

1. Give numerous characteristics—such as gestures, speech habits, and attitudes.

---

[4] From Ralph Reppert, *Ralph Reppert and his Electric Wife* (Westminster, Maryland: The Newman Press, 1963), p. 299. Reprinted by permission of the publisher.

[5] From *Taken Care Of: The Autobiography of Edith Sitwell*. Copyright © 1965 by Philip B. Frere, M.C., and Francis T. Sitwell. Reprinted by permission of Atheneum Publishers and Hutchinson & Co., Ltd.

2. Use good images (word pictures, comparisons), and give a good example of your subject in some situation.

SUGGESTED TOPICS
   my grandfather's humor, a heroine's beauty, a friend's integrity

PARAGRAPH 6

History is the recital in chronological sequence of events that are known to have occurred. Without precise chronology there can be no history, since the essence of history is the relation of events in their correct sequence. We might know something of the Battle of Marengo and something of the Battle of Waterloo, but we could not attempt to compose a history of Napoleon unless we knew which came first.   —FITZROY RICHARD SOMERSET, BARON RAGLAN[6]

ASSIGNMENT **6**

Using Paragraph 6 as your model, write a short paragraph clearly presenting a definition.

TIPS
   1. In your topic sentence, name the general class to which the word defined belongs, and mention what makes it distinctive in its class.
   2. Develop the topic by explaining the *essence*, or its distinguishing characteristic.
   3. Give a specific example to illustrate your meaning.

SUGGESTED WORDS FOR DEFINING
   sociology, miser, freshman, plutocracy, hamster, automation

PARAGRAPH 7

Convection moves heat from tropics to ice caps, and in countless places in between as well. Convection is the sea breeze that blows in toward the hot land by day, and the land breeze that heads out to sea at night, after the earth has radiated off much of its heat. Convection sends air blowing up a sunbaked mountain by day, and brings the cool mountain air down to the warm valley at night. On small scale or large, whether it is moving from walls to stove, from sea to land or from pole to equator, the net effect of convection is to move air from cooler places to warmer, and to transfer heat from warmer places to cooler.
          —PHILIP D. THOMPSON, ROBERT O'BRIEN, AND THE EDITORS OF *Life*[7]

---

[6] From Lord Raglan, "The Basis of History," *The Hero* (New York: Random House, 1956). © 1956 Fitzroy Richard Somerset, Fourth Baron Raglan. Reprinted by permission of Random House, Inc.

[7] From Philip D. Thompson, Robert O'Brien, and the editors of *Life*, *Weather* (New York: Time, Inc., 1965), p. 40. Reprinted by permission of the publisher.

ASSIGNMENT 7

Write a paragraph of about 120 words explaining a concept in terms of its applications.

TIPS

1. Before writing, compare the following dictionary definition of *convection* with the description above: "A thermal process whereby atmospheric circulation is maintained through the upward or downward transfer of air masses of different temperature."—STANDARD COLLEGE DICTIONARY
2. Be sure to use interesting specific details to clarify your concept.

SUGGESTED WORDS FOR EXPLANATION

gravity, democracy, jealousy, poverty, diplomacy, surface tension

PARAGRAPH 8

The most hopeful phenomenon occurs on the university campuses. The scholar there is more than tolerated. He is actually the hero. When I remember the mores and patterns of my own college days and compare them to those of my children, I seem to have moved onto a different planet. Football games, raccoon coats, proms and a well-bred C average were our goals and our enthusiasms. We did not read, travel, discuss the arts, listen to Bach, or extend any sympathy to those who did. But the young now are so formidably intellectual, so on fire with the love of learning, that they fill me with an amused awe. They debate books, they rush to galleries, are knowing about art, religion, philosophy, history, even metaphysics, and all with the same zeal we used to reserve for tea-dancing at the Plaza.   —PHYLLIS MC GINLEY[8]

ASSIGNMENT 8

Write a paragraph like the one above, making a comparison.

TIPS

1. Devote the first half of your paragraph to a description of one of the two persons or things or types you are comparing.
2. Devote the second half to the other side of the comparison.
3. Bring the two together in the last sentence.

SUGGESTED COMPARISONS

popular music of yesterday and today, grandmother's freedoms and mine, air travel in the forties and the sixties

---

[8] From Phyllis McGinley, "An American Cultural Renaissance," *The Critic* (February–March, 1962), p. 57. Reprinted by permission of *The Critic*.

PARAGRAPH 9

"Revolution" is doubtless a strong word, but the trend to non-ownership of automobiles is so marked that Detroit manufacturers are now competing for fleet sales to car-leasing agencies. This is not something the manufacturers like to discuss in public, although some Detroit executives privately predict the day will come when no one will own the car he drives. Even now, they say, most of the cars on the highway are not privately owned. They are rented cars, or company cars, or fleet cars leased by companies, or unpaid-for automobiles that still belong to finance companies. Leasing plans have appeared whereby dealers rent new cars to customers on a yearly basis. In return for a monthly sum, the dealer pays all costs of maintenance, including gas and oil. At the end of the year, the old car is turned in and the client leases a new one.   —JOHN KEATS[9]

ASSIGNMENT 9

Write a paragraph of about 125 words in imitation of Paragraph 9, presenting facts to back up a strongly stated topic sentence—perhaps an overstatement.

TIPS

1. For this assignment, don't be afraid to go out on a limb by way of a strong topic sentence.
2. Present details clearly and concisely.

SUGGESTED TOPICS

no home owners by 1975, wear-and-discard instead of wash-and-wear, college classes of the future, painting (music, architecture) of tomorrow

PARAGRAPH 10

The greatest hazard of all in a biological mistake is the attempt to undo it with what might turn out to be another mistake. French naturalist Roger Heim has reported how, some years ago, rabbits were released on the Macquarie Islands for food. When the rabbits began to destroy crops, officials quickly released cats to eat the rabbits. But the cats also fed on sea birds that supplied eggs which humans wanted. So dogs were brought in to chase the cats. But the dogs concentrated on the seals, also a local source of food.—GEORGE LAYCOCK[10]

ASSIGNMENT 10

Using Paragraph 10 as your model, write a paragraph giving a specific incident as convincing evidence of the truth of a generalization in the topic sentence.

---

[9] From John Keats, "Ask the Man Who *Doesn't* Own One," *Atlantic Monthly* (December, 1962), p. 64. © 1962 by John Keats. Reprinted by permission of The Sterling Lord Agency.
[10] From George Laycock, "The Animal Movers," *Sports Afield* (April, 1965), pp. 127–28. Reprinted by permission of the author and *Sports Afield*.

1. Either select one of the topic sentences below, or compose a similar one of your own.
2. Give only one incident (from history, other reading, or your own experience), with events presented chronologically.

SUGGESTED TOPIC SENTENCES

The greatest danger for a freshman is the attempt to remove his foot from his mouth.

Trying to replace one habit with another may end in a fusion of the two.

It is frustrating to try to get across a good joke that falls flat on the first telling.

PARAGRAPH 11

Many advertisers have the belief that headlines or blocks of copy on a diagonal will capture attention. Actually this is not so. Since childhood, we have been taught to read on horizontal lines. Tilting a line, therefore, slows down the reader while the eye orients itself to a new position. Anything that slows down reading is detrimental to an advertisement because it allows more distractions. Also anything that breaks the normal pace of the eye in reading—and diagonal lines definitely do that—is unpleasant for the eye and it becomes a greater task to keep receptive attention of the reader clear through the message.

—EDMUND C. ARNOLD[11]

ASSIGNMENT 11

Using Paragraph 11 as your guide, write a paragraph developed by the "straw-man method." This technique is the refutation of an idea set forth at the beginning of the paragraph.

TIPS

1. Set up your "straw man"—that is, the dummy statement to be knocked over, the idea to be disproved.
2. In the second sentence, present your opposing view.
3. Support your opinion with emphatic reasons. (For this assignment, you may invent evidence designed to upset your "straw man.")

SUGGESTED "STRAW MEN"

It is commonly believed that Mondays are blue.

Silence is golden—so they say.

"No man can be a pure specialist," writes Bernard Shaw, "without being in the strict sense an idiot."

---

[11] From Edmund C. Arnold, *Profitable Newspaper Advertising* (New York: Harper & Row, 1960), p. 21. Reprinted by permission of the publisher.

buildings. Through the bare trees, lights from smaller windows disappeared and reappeared, off and on like lightning bugs on a warm summer night; and the snow began to crunch with its new moisture, ready for a friendly snowball.

—JOSEPH E. KOKJOHN[15]

ASSIGNMENT 15

Write a short paragraph describing a scene, using Paragraph 15 as a model.

TIPS

1. Place yourself at a given position, and describe what you see from that point.
2. Select descriptive details; omit uninteresting details.
3. Arrange your description spatially—that is, according to the positions of the items you describe.

SUGGESTED TOPICS

the campus during student elections, a supermarket on double-stamp day, preparations for homecoming

PARAGRAPH 16

I began evaluating my fellow tramps as human material, and for the first time in my life I became face-conscious. There were some good faces, particularly among the young. Several of the middle-aged and the old looked healthy and well preserved. But the damaged and decayed faces were in the majority. I saw faces that were wrinkled, or bloated, or raw as the surface of a peeled plum. Some of the noses were purple and swollen, some broken, some pitted with enlarged pores. There were many toothless mouths (I counted seventy-eight). I noticed eyes that were blurred, faded, opaque, or bloodshot. I was struck by the fact that the old men, even the very old, showed their age mainly in the face. Their bodies were still slender and erect. One little man over sixty years of age looked a mere boy when seen from behind. The shriveled face joined to a boyish body made a startling sight.

—ERIC HOFFER[16]

ASSIGNMENT 16

Write a paragraph enumerating and describing what you see or hear, following the example of Paragraph 16.

TIPS

1. Limit your observations to a *part* of a whole.
2. Use effective, varied adjectives.

---

[15] From Joseph E. Kokjohn, "If Winter Comes," *Commonweal* (May 8, 1964), p. 208. Reprinted by permission of *Commonweal*.

[16] From Eric Hoffer, *The Ordeal of Change* (New York: Harper & Row, 1952), pp. 140–41. Reprinted by permission of the publisher.

SUGGESTED TOPICS
smiles, hair styles, voices, table manners

PARAGRAPH 17

Most diamonds are found in a rock known as blue ground, or kimberlite, and must undergo extensive processing. On the average, some twenty tons of rock or gravel must be processed to yield diamonds totaling four carats. Fewer than half of these will be worth cutting as gems; the remainder are used industrially. Cutting reduces the weight by half, again. As a general rule, the diamond miners have to dig, blast and crush more than 250 tons of ore to find a natural stone large enough to yield a one-carat cut diamond. —MERRILL POLLACK[17]

ASSIGNMENT 17

Using Paragraph 17 as your model, write an explanatory paragraph with organized details.

TIPS
1. Put into your first sentence the topic to be explained.
2. Develop the topic by factual information dealing with key words in your first sentence (such as *diamonds* and *extensive processing* in Paragraph 17).
3. Organize your facts, placing them in climactic order and ending with a strong, memorable point.

SUGGESTED TOPICS
the making of a spider web, the creation of a stained-glass window, what goes into a bale of cotton (or hay)

PARAGRAPH 18

Just under three hundred years ago, the Lucasian Professor of Mathematics at Cambridge did a distinctly unusual thing. He decided that one of his pupils was a much better mathematician than he was, and in all respects more fitted for his job. He wasn't content with this exercise in self-criticism. He promptly resigned his Chair, on condition that his pupil be immediately appointed. In the light of history, no one can say that his judgment was wrong. For the Professor's name was Barrow, and he was a very good mathematician by seventeenth-century standards; but his pupil was Isaac Newton. —C. P. SNOW[18]

---

[17] From Merrill Pollack, "Holiday Handbook of Precious Stone," *Holiday* (March, 1963), p. 156. © 1963 The Curtis Publishing Company. Reprinted by permission of *Holiday*.

[18] From C. P. Snow, "On Magnanimity," *Harper's Magazine* (July, 1962), p. 37. Reprinted by permission of *Harper's Magazine*.

Describe an incident leading to a surprise ending.

TIPS

1. Give key words (like *distinctly unusual*) in the first sentence suggesting the ending and giving focus to the entire paragraph.
2. Use only those narrative details that are pertinent to the final surprise sentence.

SUGGESTED ENDINGS

That boy was my father (Abe Lincoln, Orville Wright, Henry Longfellow).
Thus the villain became the hero.
The wallet (box, tank, refrigerator, envelope) was empty.

PARAGRAPH 19

To cut a piece of glass tubing (or rod), make a scratch with a rapid *forward* motion of a triangular file at the point at which the tubing is to be cut. Immediately grasp the tubing with both hands (one on each side of the scratch); hold the tubing so that the scratch is on the opposite side from your body, and lightly press the glass outward, with the ends of your thumbs near the scratch, while simultaneously pulling the ends away from each other and toward your body. The tubing will snap where you made the scratch because the friction of the file against the glass produces a temporary strain in the structure of the glass. If the break is uneven it is probably because you did not apply pressure uniformly with your fingers and thumbs. You can break off small projections of glass by rubbing a wire gauze briskly over their tips.   —LAWRENCE P. EBLIN[19]

ASSIGNMENT 19

Write a paragraph giving clear instructions or directions.

TIPS

1. Begin with an infinitive phrase stating what is to be done.
2. Give the steps of the procedure in the proper order.

SUGGESTED TOPICS

how to park parallel, how to make a collage, how to eat spaghetti (lobster)

PARAGRAPH 20

Who is a necrophilous person?
He is one who is attracted to and fascinated by all that is not alive, to all that

---

[19] From Lawrence P. Eblin, *The Elements of Chemistry in the Laboratory* (New York: Harcourt, Brace & World, 1965), pp. 3–4. Reprinted by permission of the publisher.

is dead; to corpses, to decay, to feces, to dirt. Necrophiles are those people who love to talk about sickness, burials, death. They come to life precisely when they can talk about death. A clear example of the pure necrophilous type was Hitler. He was fascinated by destruction, and the smell of death was sweet to him. While in the years of success it may have appeared that he wanted only to destroy those whom he considered his enemies, the days of the *Götterdämmerung* at the end showed that his deepest satisfaction lay in witnessing total and absolute destruction: that of the German people, of those around him, of himself.

—ERICH FROMM[20]

ASSIGNMENT 20

First ask a question beginning with *who* or *what*. Then, with Paragraph 20 as your model, answer the question, using about 125 words.

TIPS
    1. Begin your answer in general terms, swiftly moving to specifics.
    2. Next, present a clear illustration.

SUGGESTED QUESTIONS
    Who is an optimist (an opera buff, an intellectual)?
    Who is a philanthropist? (an introvert? a hypochondriac?)

PARAGRAPH 21

In the freedom of the scientific world individuality thrives and stereotypes wilt. Some scientists serve humanity self-effacingly; others are flamboyant egotists. Some are convivial souls who like to rub shoulders and tell jokes; others play the misanthrope, wishing well only of minerals, vegetables and more nearly extinct species of animals. One scientist may scoff at religion, while another prays daily for guidance. One may read nothing but technical periodicals and the Sunday comics, while another quotes Dante or Shakespeare like an Oxford don. One may wear loafers and substitute talcum powder for socks, while another is always turned out as impeccably as a banker.

—HENRY MARGENAU, DAVID BERGAMINI, AND THE EDITORS OF *Life*[21]

ASSIGNMENT 21

With Paragraph 21 as your model, write about 100 words making a contrast.

---

[20] From Erich Fromm, *The Heart of Man* (New York: Harper & Row, 1964), p. 39. Reprinted by permission of the publisher.
[21] From Henry Margenau, David Bergamini, and the editors of *Life*, *The Scientist* (New York: Time, Inc., 1964), pp. 31–32. Reprinted by permission of the publisher.

1. Put your topic sentence first.
2. Develop this topic by making a specific contrast in each sentence—using such paired words as *some . . . others, one . . . another.*
3. Use parallel sentence structure.

SUGGESTED TOPICS

individuality among shoppers, varieties of parental supervision, individual styles of comedians

PARAGRAPH 22

Roughly, satire has two main methods. The method of Juvenal and Sinclair Lewis and Dickens is to attack furiously with blunderbuss or cudgel. That is direct satire. The other is more roundabout. Instead of meeting the foe upon the field it may pretend to be a neutral and undermine him by suave and diplomatic ways. It may masquerade as a friend or as one of his own defenders and insidiously destroy his faith in himself. Such is the strategy of Anatole France and, in milder vein, of Jane Austen. It is indirect satire. —EDGAR JOHNSON[22]

ASSIGNMENT 22

Using the paragraph above as your model, write about 75 words setting forth a classification.

TIPS

1. In your topic sentence, give your key word (like *satire,* above) and the number (only two or three) of your classifications.
2. Explain each classification (like *direct satire* and *indirect satire*) by pointing out distinguishing characteristics, using specific references or facts.
3. Relate the classifications to each other as you define each class.

SUGGESTED TOPICS

two kinds of insults, simple irony and dramatic irony, types of football fans

---

[22] From Edgar Johnson, *A Treasury of Satire* (New York: Simon and Schuster, 1945), p. 93. Copyright 1945 by Edgar Johnson. Reprinted by permission of the author.

REVIEW EXERCISE

Every novel must do one of three things—it must (1) tell something, (2) show something, or (3) prove something. Some novels do all three of these; some do only two; all must do at least one. The ordinary novel merely tells something, elaborates a complication, devotes itself primarily to *things*. In this class comes the novel of adventure, such as *The Three Musketeers*. The second and better class of novel shows something, exposes the workings of a temperament, devotes itself primarily to the minds of human beings. In this class falls the novel of character, such as *Romola*. The third, and what we hold to be the best class, proves something, draws conclusions from a whole congeries of forces, social tendencies, race impulses, devotes itself not to the study of men but of man. In this class falls the novel with a purpose, such as *Les Miserables*. —FRANK NORRIS[23]

I. Answer the following questions:

1. What are the first and last words of the topic sentence of the paragraph above? _____

2. Does the author develop his topic by classification, by examples, by definition, by explanatory details—or by a combination of these methods?

   _____

3. Is the second sentence a clear statement of the controlling idea, or does it relate the three classifications? _____

   _____

4. Is the definition of the ordinary novel parallel in structure to the definition of the novel that shows something? _____

5. What is the example of the ordinary novel? _____

   _____

6. What part of speech (verb, adverb, noun) ends each sentence defining each class? _____

7. Does the example *Romola* follow or precede the clarification of the second type of novel? _____

---

23 From Frank Norris, *The Responsibilities of the Novelist* (New York: Doubleday, 1903).

8. Does the author use parallel sentence structure in presenting all three examples? _____

9. Are the three classes presented in order of importance? _____

10. Do the words *second* and *third* and *better* and *best* serve as transitional words? _____

11. What word in the topic sentence appears several times in the paragraph?

_____

12. What word not in the topic sentence appears five times? _____

13. Does repetition of words and of sentence patterns contribute to the unity, the organization, of ideas? _____

14. Does the paragraph lead into a clincher sentence restating the topic sentence? _____

15. Is every sentence in the paragraph directly related to the controlling idea? _____

1. *Every, something* 2. *a combination* 3. *relates the classifications* 4. *yes* 5. The Three Musketeers 6. *noun* 7. *follow* 8. *yes* 9. *yes* 10. *yes* 11. *novel* 12. *class* 13. *yes* 14. *no* 15. *yes*

II. Write a paragraph using a combination of methods for development, giving special attention to organization. Use the paragraph by Frank Norris as your model.

STEPS

    1. In your topic sentence, which will come first in your paragraph, enumerate three closely related ideas for developing.
    2. Decide upon clear definitions or explanations of these three points.
    3. Carefully select an example for each point.
    4. Decide upon the most effective order of presentation of the three points.
    5. Use repetition of words and of sentence patterns effectively.

SUGGESTED SUBJECTS

    A good teacher (quarterback, president, watchdog, stoic) always does one of three things. Every museum (library, park, college, state fair) must have one of three things. Operas (baseball series, college calendars, mysteries) must include one of three things.

part **III**

**A SELF-TEACHING REVIEW
OF GRAMMAR**

1

NONSENTENCES	SENTENCES
a. Warren!	d. Warren bristled.
b. that soft soap	e. Is that soft soap?
c. me from Pecksniffs	f. Preserve me from Pecksniffs!
Every grammatically complete sentence has a verb.	

1. What word in *d* converts *a* to a sentence? _____

2. What word in *e* is the verb? _____

3. What verb in *f* makes a sentence of *c*? _____

1. *bristled*   2. *Is*   3. *Preserve*

A change in a verb's position may convert a statement to a question or to an exclamation.

Wayne *is* her partner.   *Is* Wayne her partner?
My face *was* red.   *Was* my face red!

QUICK QUIZ

A. She cast a shadow like a long bird's.   —THE ATLANTIC MONTHLY
B. The most pleasant interruption in the world!   —THE ATLANTIC MONTHLY

1. What is the verb in *A*? _____

2. Is *B* a grammatically complete sentence? _____

1. *cast*   2. *no*

2

SUBJECTS	SUBJECTS WITH VERBS
plans	a. The plans backfired.
Chester	b. Chester often flips a coin.
ship	c. Is that ship seaworthy?
you, she	d. Have you and she any suggestions?
A verb makes, or helps make, an assertion or inquiry about its subject, which names the one (ones) doing, being, or having.	

1. What verb in *a* makes an assertion about *plans?* _____

2. Does the verb in *b* help make an assertion about Chester? _____

3. Does *Is* in *c* help make an inquiry about *ship?* _____

4. What is the verb in *d* ? _____

1. *backfired*   2. *yes*   3. *yes*   4. *Have*

Often the verb is grammatically linked to its subject by its form.

He watches. They watch.   Have I won? Has she won?

QUICK QUIZ

The earth roared and heaved and shook. Acrid gases permeated the air while the yellow sunlight turned abruptly to a brassy overcast.   —HARPER'S MAGAZINE

1. The verbs *roared, heaved,* and *shook* make an assertion about what subject?

_____

2. Name the verbs in the second sentence. _____

1. *earth*   2. *permeated, turned*

3

PRINCIPAL VERBS	VERB PHRASES
practice helping seen	a. The choir must practice. b. Should she be helping Junior? c. Flying saucers may have been seen.
A verb phrase consists of more than one word: the principal verb accompanied by one or more auxiliaries or verb helpers.	

1. What auxiliary accompanies the principal verb in *a?* _____

2. In *b*, what auxiliaries accompany *helping?* _____

3. In *c*, what is the verb phrase? _____

1. *must*   2. *Should be*   3. *may have been seen*

The following words are commonly used as auxiliaries in verb phrases: *be, being, been, am, is, are, was, were, has, have, had, do, does, did, can, could, may, might, shall, should, will, would, must.*

A verb phrase may be interrupted by a word or words not a part of the verb phrase: "The mail *had* not yet *come.*"

QUICK QUIZ

Her strategy was attack, forever attack, with one baffling departure: she might sacrifice certain tricks as expendable if only she could have the last ones, the heartbreaking ones, if she could slap them down one after another, shatteringly.

—J. F. POWERS

1. Is there a verb phrase used before the colon? _____

2. Write the verb phrases used after the colon. _____

_____

1. *no*   2. *might sacrifice, could have, could slap*

4

VERBS	VERB EQUIVALENTS
a. Fay resembles her dad.	f. Fay takes after her dad.
b. I came for coffee.	g. I dropped over for coffee.
c. He disinherited Elmer.	h. He cut Elmer off.
Some word groups are equivalent to single verbs.	

1. In *f*, what is the equivalent of the verb in *a*? _____

2. In *b*, what verb takes the place of *dropped over*? _____

3. In *h*, what is the equivalent of the verb in *c*? _____

1. *takes after*   2. *came*   3. *cut off*

The meaning, not the form, of a word determines whether or not it is a verb equivalent.

SINGLE-WORD VERBS	VERB EQUIVALENTS
I *jumped* on the trampoline.	I *jumped on* him. (scolded)
He *ran* across the campus.	He *ran across* an old friend.

QUICK QUIZ

The tycoon of great-grandfather's day simply foreclosed on his friends, waved them off to the poorhouse, then put on a fresh collar and dropped in at Delmonico's to make some new friends.

—W. F. MIKSCH

1. What is the verb equivalent of *donned*? _____

2. What is the verb equivalent of *visited*? _____

1. *put on*   2. *dropped in*

5

AUXILIARIES	AUXILIARY EQUIVALENTS
will (shall) eat	is going to (was going to) eat, am to (were to) eat, is about to eat
must eat	has to (have to) eat
were eating	used to eat, kept on eating
should eat	ought to eat, had better eat
Some word groups are equivalent to single auxiliaries.	

1. *Is going to* may serve as the equivalent of what single-word auxiliary?

_____

2. What single-word auxiliary means *ought to?* _____

1. *will (shall)* 2. *should*

Meaning, not form, determines whether or not a word group is an auxiliary equivalent.

VERBS	AUXILIARY EQUIVALENTS
I *am going* to the dance.	I *am going to* dance. (*will* dance)
The fish *will keep* on ice.	The fish *will keep on* biting.

QUICK QUIZ

A. Mother used to send a box of candy every Christmas to the people in the Airedale bit.
　　　　　　　　　　　　　　　　　　　　　　　—JAMES THURBER

B. I'm not going to arrive at nineteen as long as my mother remains at thirty-seven.
　　　　　　　　　　　　　　　　　　　　—SAKI (H. H. MUNRO)

1. Is *used to* above an auxiliary equivalent? _____

2. What auxiliary equivalent means *will* or *shall?* _____

1. *yes* 2. *am going to*

6

TIME	CHANGES IN VERB FORMS
present	We sing. We are singing. It is sung. We do sing. We can sing. We keep on singing.
past	We sang. We were singing. It was sung. We did sing. We kept on singing. We used to sing. We have sung. We had sung. We were going to sing.
future	We will (shall) sing. It will be sung. We will be singing. We are going to sing. We are to sing. We are about to sing.
Every verb can be conjugated, changing its form to show time.	

1. What change in *sing* can convert that verb to the past? _____

2. What change in the auxiliary can convert *do sing* to the past? _____

3. What auxiliary equivalent can be used with *we sing* to indicate the immediate future? _____

1. *sang*   2. *did*   3. *are about to*

The conventional conjugation of a verb involves six tenses.

present tense:	I seldom *sing* it now. (He seldom *sings*.)
past tense:	I *sang* it last week.
future tense:	I *shall (will) sing* it tomorrow.
present perfect tense:	I *have sung* it before now. (He *has sung*.)
past perfect tense:	I *had sung* it before last week.
future perfect tense:	I *shall (will) have sung* it before tomorrow.

(See the conjugation of *be*, page 213.)

QUICK QUIZ

Our big campuses are churning in a traffic turmoil that almost has to be seen to be believed. Some schools—Indiana is one—issue stickers, dubbed "hunting licenses," which permit the student to park on campus if he can find a space.

—JEROME ELLISON

1. The verbs above are consistently in what tense? _____

2. What verbs show time without using auxiliaries? _____

_____

3. What auxiliaries indicate time? _____

1. *present*   2. *is, issue, permit*   3. *are, has to be, can*

7

SUBJECTS OTHER THAN THIRD-PERSON SINGULAR	THIRD-PERSON-SINGULAR SUBJECTS
a. I blame her.	e. She blames her.
b. Strangers ask Jim that.	f. Don asks Jim that.
c. Flowers grow here.	g. The flower grows here.
d. Have you any money?	h. Has he any money?
In the present tense, every verb changes its form to indicate a singular subject in the third person.	

1. Changing *I* to *She* converts *blame* to what? _____

2. What ending is added to *ask* for the subject *Don?* _____

3. When *s* is added to *grow*, what number is the subject? _____

4. The subject *he* in *h* changes *have* to what? _____

1. *blames*   2. *-s*   3. *singular*   4. *has*

Singular number means one; *plural,* more than one. Though we speak of a "singular verb" or a "plural verb," we are actually referring to the number of the verb's subject.

> *singular subjects:* I have. You have. It has.
> *plural subjects:*   We have. You have. Several have.

The *-s* ending on a present verb indicates that its subject is both singular and in the third person. *I ask. He asks.*

Every subject has *person*—first, second, or third.

> *First person (speaking):*   I, we
> *Second person (spoken to):*   you
> *Third person (spoken about):* he, she, one, it, they

QUICK QUIZ

In the best of these stories there is a moment of madness when the protagonist discovers that his knowledge of the world falls short of its final horror.

—JONATHAN BAUMBACH

1. What is the subject of *discovers?* _____

2. What is the person and number of the subject of *falls?* _____

_____

3. What is the subject of *falls?* _____

1. *protagonist*   2. *third, singular*   3. *knowledge*

8

INFINITIVE	PAST	PAST PARTICIPLE	PRESENT PARTICIPLE
place	placed	placed	placing
write	wrote	written	writing
burst	burst	burst	bursting

Basic forms of a verb are the infinitive, the past, the past participle, and the present participle.

1. What is the past form of *place?* _____

2. What is the past-participle form of *write?* _____

3. What ending marks the present-participle form? _____

1. *placed*   2. *written*   3. *-ing*

The **infinitive form** is that form used with *to:* to *place,* to *write,* to *burst.* As a verb, the infinitive form without *to* is used for the present tense; with a third-person singular subject, the *-s* is added: *I write. He writes.* This infinitive form is also used with auxiliaries such as *will, do, can, may,* and *must,* as well as those ending in *to: I will write. He did write. You ought to write.* (For uses of the infinitive form in the imperative and subjunctive moods, see pages 215–16.) With *to,* this verb form functions both as a noun and as a modifier (see page 230).

The **past form** is that form of the verb which is always used without an auxiliary to indicate simple past tense: *I wrote. It burst yesterday. He placed it there.*

The **past-participle form** may function both as an adjective (see participle, page 251) and as a verb. As a verb, the past-participle form is always accompanied by *has, have, had,* or a form of *be: I have written. It was written.*

The **present-participle form** may function as an adjective (see page 251), as a noun (see page 229), and as a verb. As a verb, the present-participle form is always accompanied by a form of *be* (or *keep on*): *I am writing now. He will be writing to you. He kept on writing.*

QUICK QUIZ

The voices had toned away to mere whisperings. The drummer wished to ask further questions, which were born of an increasing anxiety and bewilderment; but when he attempted them, the men merely looked at him in irritation and motioned him to remain silent.   —STEPHEN CRANE

1. How many simple-past verb forms are used above? _____

2. List each past-participle verb form with its auxiliary. _____

---

1. *four*   2. *had toned, were born*

9

INFINITIVE FORM	PAST FORM	PAST-PARTICIPLE FORM
We use coal. Jo will ask.	We used coal. Jo asked.	We have used coal. Jo has asked.
The past form and the past-participle form of a regular verb consist of the infinitive form with the ending *-d* or *-ed.*		

1. What ending is added to the infinitive form of the first verb to change it to the past? _____

2. What ending puts *ask* in the past form? _____

3. Does the past-participle form of a regular verb differ from its past form?

_____

1. *-d* 2. *-ed* 3. *no*

A few regular verbs have two acceptable forms for the past and the past participle: *burned, burnt—leaped, leapt—kneeled, knelt.*

QUICK QUIZ

A. Well, someday has arrived!   —SATURDAY REVIEW
B. The best writers and critics of the eighteenth century despised Defoe. His public loved him.   —HORIZON

1. In *A*, what is the past-participle form in the verb phrase? _____

2. In *B*, what ending is added to the infinitive forms of both verbs? _____

3. Are all the verbs above regular? _____

1. *arrived* 2. *-d* 3. *yes*

10

INFINITIVE FORM	PAST FORM	PAST-PARTICIPLE FORM
I begin late.	I began late.	I have begun late.
It may not cut.	It cut well.	It was cut by him.
Come here.	He came here.	He has come here.
Paul will go.	Paul went early.	Paul had gone early.

The past form and the past-participle form of an irregular verb do not consist of the infinitive form with *-d* or *-ed.*

1. Which verb has a vowel change in each form? _____

2. Which verb above does not change its spelling? _____

3. Which verb shows the most radical change in the past? _____

4. Do any verbs above other than *cut* have the same form for both past and past participle? _____

1. *begin* 2. *cut* 3. *go* 4. *no*

Unlike regular verbs, nearly all irregular verbs have different forms for the past and the past participle.

Some verbs have two correct forms, one regular and the other irregular:

show, showed, (have) shown or *(have) showed*
dive, dived or *dove, (have) dived*

QUICK QUIZ

She kicked her foot over the furrow, and with mouth drawn down shook her head once or twice in a little strutting way. Some husks blew down and whirled in streamers about her skirts.　　　　　—EUDORA WELTY

1. In the first sentence, what irregular verb is in the past form? _____

2. What is the irregular verb in the second sentence? _____

1. *shook*　2. *blew*

11

	SINGULAR SUBJECTS	PLURAL SUBJECTS
present	I am, you are, he is	we, you, they are
past	I was, you were, he was	we, you, they were
future	I, you, he will be	we, you, they will be
present perfect	I have been, you have been, he has been	we, you, they have been
past perfect	I, you, he had been	we, you, they had been
future perfect	I, you, he will have been	we, you, they will have been

The forms of *be* are *be, am, is, are, was, were, being,* and *been.*

1. How many forms of *be* indicate present tense? _____

2. What are the forms of *be* in the simple past? _____

3. In a verb phrase, does *been* always have an auxiliary? _____

1. *three*　2. *was, were*　3. *yes*

Forms of *be* may function as single verbs or as the principal verb in verb phrases.

single verb:　　　　　　　*Were* you there?
principal verb in a phrase: She *has been* thrifty.

Be is frequently used as a linking verb, which connects the subject with the subject complement. In the example above, the linking verb *has been* connects the subject *she* with the subject complement *thrifty*. (See pages 231–32 for a discussion of the subject complement.)

In verb phrases, a form of *be* is used with present-participle forms:

They *are televising* the movie.   *Is* he *being* discreet?

Be is the most frequently used and the most irregular verb in the language: *be* changes with a shift of subject (*I am, you are, he is*); it is freakish in its various tenses (*I am, I will be*); it even takes a form of itself as its own auxiliary (*was being*).

QUICK QUIZ

As a rule, I try not to look into mirrors any more than is absolutely necessary. Things are depressing enough as they are without my going out of my way to make myself miserable.   —ROBERT BENCHLEY

1. Name all the forms of *be* used in the paragraph above. _____

2. How would these forms change if the past tense had been consistently used?

_____

1. *is, are*   2. *was, were*

12

ACTIVE VOICE	PASSIVE VOICE
a. We ask questions.	d. Questions are asked.
b. Were they drinking tea?	e. Hot tea was being drunk.
c. I broke the record.	f. The record got broken.

A verb in the passive voice has at least one form of *be* (or *get*) plus a past participle; the object of a verb in the active voice becomes subject when the verb is made passive.

1. In *a*, what is object of the verb *ask*? _____

2. In *d*, what is subject of the verb *are asked*? _____

3. In *b*, is *were* followed by a past participle? _____

4. In *e*, is *was being* followed by a past participle? _____
1. *questions*   2. *Questions*   3. *no*   4. *yes*

Like an "eye rhyme" (*though, enough*), which *looks like* but does not sound like a rhyme, a structure may *look like* but not have the meaning of the passive.

> *real passive:*   He was tried by a jury. (*meaning:* The jury tried him.)
> *"eye passive":* He was very collected. (*meaning:* He was very calm.)

Other verbs do not *look like* passives, since they do not have a form of *be* (or *get*) plus a past participle, but are implicitly passive—that is, the passive *meaning* is clearly understood, though not specifically expressed by form.

> *real passive:* That newly varnished table was scratched by me.
> *implicit passive:* That newly varnished table scratches easily.
> (*meaning:* The table can be scratched easily.)

QUICK QUIZ

Now we are asked to decide whether an innocent and inoffensive man may exercise the right of self-defense against society itself, when the society has been not arbitrary but only misguided, not malicious, but only mistaken.   —SHOW

1. What is the real passive verb? _____

2. Are *misguided* and *mistaken* parts of an "eye passive" or of an implicit

   passive or of a real passive? _____

1. *are asked*   2. *"eye passive"*

13

INDICATIVE MOOD	IMPERATIVE MOOD
a. Men hated tyranny. b. Will you please stop?	c. Hate tyranny! d. Please stop.

In the indicative mood, a verb has varying forms and subjects.

In the imperative mood, a verb has only the infinitive form and only one subject, seldom expressed: *you.*

1. In *a*, what verb is used? What tense is it? _____

2. In *a*, what is the subject of *hated*? In *c*, of *Hate*? _____

3. In *d*, what words are dropped to change the indicative verb in *b* to the

   imperative? _____

1. *hated, past*   2. *Men, you*   3. *Will you*

The indicative mood is used for making statements or asking questions. The imperative mood expresses a command or a request. An imperative verb can stand alone as a sentence. *Look. Stop!*

The same sentence may contain both indicative and imperative verbs.

> Herman said, "Open the window."
> Think about it, and you will agree with me.

One of the most helpful aids in developing a good memory is the determination to be cautious in learning new knowledge and habits. Do things *right* at the start. Concentrate on accuracy, not speed, at the beginning. And get a coach, if necessary. —JAMES D. WEINLAND

1. Is the verb in the first sentence in the indicative or the imperative? _____

   _____

2. List the verbs in the imperative mood. _____

   _____

3. What is the subject of these verbs? _____

1. *indicative*   2. *Do, Concentrate, get*   3. *you*

14

INDICATIVE MOOD	SUBJUNCTIVE MOOD
a. He is not rich. b. I am not single. c. He goes to work late.	d. He acts as if he *were* rich. e. I wish I *were* single. f. She insists that he *go* to work.

Verb forms in the subjunctive mood are used to indicate a condition contrary to fact, a wish, a supposition, a demand.

1. In *a*, the indicative *is* changes to what form in *d*? _____

2. In *a* and *b*, does the verb form differ for *he* and *I*? _____

3. In *d* and *e*, does the verb form differ in the subjunctive for the subjects

   he and *I*? _____

4. The indicative *goes* changes to what in the subjunctive after the verb *insists?*

   _____

1. *were*   2. *yes*   3. *no*   4. *go*

In the subjunctive mood, the verb form is the same for every subject.

> *subjunctive:* I were, you were, he were, we were, they were
> I be, you be, he be, we be, they be

If and *even if* may precede an indicative or a subjunctive verb, depending on the meaning.

216   a self-teaching review of grammar

indicative: Even if it *was* snowing, we enjoyed our hike. (It actually was snowing.)
subjunctive: If it *were* snowing, we would build an igloo. (It is not snowing.)

In both informal and formal usage, the subjunctive form seems to be dying out.

I wish there was something I could do.—RAY BRADBURY

QUICK QUIZ

A. All around, it is as if the world were stilled into silence, and time blended into eternity.   —STEPHEN LEACOCK
B. Such a school demands from the teacher that he be a kind of artist in his province.   —ALBERT EINSTEIN

1. In *A*, what is the first subjunctive verb phrase? _____

2. In *A*, is the understood verb with *blended* indicative or subjunctive? _____

_____

3. In *B*, what subjunctive verb follows *demands?* _____

1. *were stilled*   2. *subjunctive*   3. *be*

REVIEW EXERCISE A

1. Must every grammatically complete sentence have a verb? _____

2. In the sentence that follows, are both *am* and *likes* linked grammatically to their subjects? *I am sure that she likes me.* _____

3. A verb phrase consists of one or more auxiliaries plus what? _____

   _____

4. What determines whether or not a word group is a verb equivalent—form or meaning? _____

5. *Used to* and *ought to* are what type of equivalent in *used to go* and *ought to go?* _____

6. Can every verb in the language change its form (by spelling or by auxiliary) to indicate tense? _____

7. What auxiliary accompanies the principal verb in the past perfect tense?

   _____

8. Is *ask* a regular or an irregular verb? _____

9. Is *come* a regular or an irregular verb? _____

10. How many forms does *be* have? _____

11. Is the verb in the following sentence a real passive, or is it an eye passive? *He was tried by a jury.* _____

12. What ending on an infinitive form of a verb indicates a singular subject in the third person? _____

13. Does a verb in the simple past tense ever have an auxiliary? _____

14. In the past tense, regular verbs end in what? _____

15. Do the simple-past form and the past-participle form of a regular verb differ? _____

16. Can the infinitive form of every verb in the language take the -ing ending?

_____

17. As a part of a verb phrase, must a present participle be accompanied by a form of be or keep? _____

18. A verb in the passive voice consists of a past participle plus a form of what?

_____

19. What form of a verb is always used for the imperative mood? _____

_____

20. The indicative was changes in the subjunctive mood to what? _____

_____

1. yes   2. yes   3. principal verb   4. meaning   5. auxiliary   6. yes   7. had   8. regular
9. irregular   10. eight   11. real   12. -s   13. no   14. -d or -ed   15. no   16. yes   17. yes
18. be (or get)   19. infinitive   20. were

REVIEW EXERCISE B

1. *Tom is always threatening to grow a beard.* What word could be shifted to the beginning to change the statement to a question? _____

2. *At ten every morning, I zoom into Ed's driveway.* If *I* were changed to *he*, how would the verb be written? _____

3. (a) *He eats four meals.* (b) *Should he do so?* Which sentence contains a verb phrase, *a* or *b*? _____

4. *Clara passed out when Peter was tackled hard.* What word group is equivalent to a single verb? _____

5. *Mr. Rodie is going to make reservations.* What word group is equivalent to *will?* _____

6. *Today Greg is tinkering with his motorcycle.* If *Today* were *Yesterday,* *is* would change to what? _____

7. *When you aim, you always hit the mark.* If each *you* were a *he,* what would the verbs be? _____

8. *There have been rumors.* If *rumors* were *gossip,* what would *have* change to?

_____

9. *They believe whatever they hear.* What letter added to the verbs would put this sentence in the past tense? _____

10. *She had kneeled. She had knelt.* Are both verbs correct? _____

11. *The pipes burst in freezing weather.* If *last year* were added, would the verb change? _____

12. *Are you as happy as I am that they will be here?* How many forms of *be* are used? _____

13. *Too often has Pete been told that he is lazy.* (a) What form of *be* stands as a single verb? _____

    (b) What form of *be* functions as an auxiliary? _____

14. *Are river towns dreading spring thaws?* What form of *be* is used with *dreading?* _____

15. (a) *The saucer was dirty and cracked.* (b) *The pane was cracked by hail.* Which has the real passive verb, *a* or *b?* _____

16. *I know that I ought to accept the gifts.* What are the infinitive verb forms?

_____

17. *Had he left before the doctor came?* What verb is in the simple past tense?

_____

18. *I ran an errand that Sid had forgotten.* What verb is in the past perfect tense? _____

19. (a) *When I call, Jim answers me.* (b) *When I call, Jim, answer me.* Which sentence has a verb in the imperative, *a* or *b*? _____

20. *I demand that he make reparation.* Which verb is in the subjunctive mood?

_____

1. *is*   2. *zooms*   3. *b*   4. *passed out*   5. *is going to*   6. *was*   7. *aims, hits*   8. *has*   9. *d*
10. *yes*   11. *no*   12. *three*   13. (a) *is,* (b) *been*   14. *are*   15. *b*   16. *know, accept*   17. *came*
18. *had forgotten*   19. *b*   20. *make*

nouns and noun substitutes 2

1

NOUNS
a. The *cows* belong to a *Mr. Ransom*. b. Consider the *acts* and *reliability* of the *baby sitter*.
Nouns designate whoever or whatever can be discussed.

1. In *a*, *who* owns the cow? *What* are owned? _____

2. In *a*, what words immediately precede the nouns? _____

3. In *b*, can *acts* and *reliability* be discussed? _____

4. In *b*, what two words function as a single noun?_____

1. *Mr. Ransom, cows* 2. *The, a* 3. *yes* 4. *baby sitter*

Ordinarily, nouns designate or name persons, places, things, animals, ideas, or actions. *A, an,* and *the* are noun markers: a *remark*, an interesting *silence*, the *Fergusons*. Two or more words may function as a single (or compound) noun: *necktie, cottage cheese, Miss Evans, mother-in-law, do-gooder*.

Many nouns have characteristic endings, such as *-ation, -sion, -ance, -ism, -ist, -ity, -ment*, and *-ness: recommendation, resistance, defeatism, determinist, integrity*.

Nouns may or may not be capitalized.

> I want you to meet my only *sister, Caroline*.
> This *university* could become another *Harvard*.

QUICK QUIZ

The dawn came quickly now, a wash, a glow, a lightness, and then an explosion of fire as the sun arose out of the Gulf. —JOHN STEINBECK

1. *The* signals what three nouns? _____

2. What endings convert the verb forms *light* and *explode* to nouns? _____

_____

3. Are *wash, glow,* and *fire* verbs or nouns? _____

4. How many nouns are in Steinbeck's sentence? _____

1. *dawn, sun, Gulf* 2. *-ness, -sion* 3. *nouns* 4. *eight*

2

SINGULAR	PLURAL
a. Jay welcomed the guest.	e. Jay welcomed the guests.
b. Did an Iowan speak?	f. Did the Iowans speak?
c. His son-in-law called.	g. His sons-in-law called.
d. The sheep was black.	h. The sheep were black.

The form of nearly all nouns indicates singular or plural.

1. What ending converts three nouns to plural? _____

2. What capitalized noun is made plural with -s? _____

3. In g, what word in the compound noun takes -s? _____

4. In d and h, does *sheep* by its form show number? _____

1. -s   2. *Iowans*   3. *sons*   4. *no*

Most nouns form the plural by adding -s or -es.

> *singular:* clam, idea, glass, church
> *plural:*   clams, ideas, glasses, churches

When a compound noun is written as one word, it forms the plural by adding -s or -es; when it is written separately or hyphenated, the key word is pluralized.

> *singular:* carload, disk jockey, man about town, mother-in-law, double-decker
> *plural:*   carloads, disk jockeys, men about town, mothers-in-law, double-deckers

The plurals of a few nouns are formed in irregular ways: *woman, women; child, children; mouse, mice.* Some nouns do not change form to indicate number. Some noun forms can be singular or plural; other nouns can be singular only or plural only.

> *singular or plural:* sheep, deer, measles, Chinese
> *singular only:*   God, wisdom, World War I, integrity, homesickness
> *plural only:*   people, clothes, pliers, twins, remains, cattle

QUICK QUIZ

Though there was a growing skepticism concerning her ability to "throw spells" or work love charms, even Mrs. Oakley admitted her success in removing moles and warts and in making cows go dry at the wrong season.   —ELLEN GLASGOW

1. Is *spells* a noun or a verb? _____

2. Besides *love charms*, what is the other compound noun? _____

3. How many nouns above have a final -*s* for plural? _____

1. *noun*   2. *Mrs. Oakley*   3. *five*

3

UNINFLECTED NOUNS	SINGULAR	PLURAL
home owned by the mayor	the mayor's home	the mayors' homes
worth a dollar	a dollar's worth	ten dollars' worth
books for a child	a child's books	children's books
voice of a lady	a lady's voice	some ladies' voices
car of his son-in-law	his son-in-law's car	his sons-in-law's cars

A noun changes its form to show possession or relationship.

1. What mark of punctuation and letter substitute for *owned by?* _____

2. Does the -*'s* in *dollar's* show ownership? _____

3. What two words above have the apostrophe before the -*s* in the plural?

_____

4. For plural nouns ending in -*s* or -*es*, does the apostrophe come before or after

the -*s?* _____

1. -*'s* (or -*s'*)   2. *no*   3. *children's, sons-in-law's*   4. *after*

When there is joint ownership, the apostrophe is used only for the last noun: *Vernon and Frank's boat.*

Note: When words, figures, and symbols are italicized (or underlined), the apostrophe may be used to show plural number only: "The *a's* in my *and's* look like *o's.*"

QUICK QUIZ

I followed a footpath and descended to the water's edge. The pond lay clear and blue in the morning light, as you have seen it so many times. In the shallows a man's waterlogged shirt undulated gently.   —E. B. WHITE

1. Which noun indicates ownership? _____

2. Which noun indicates relationship? _____

3. If these nouns were plural, how would they be written?_____

_____

1. *man's*   2. *water's*   3. *waters', men's*

4

NOUNS	PRONOUNS
a. The boys passed the test. b. Cheating is frowned upon. c. Ed is a buyer. Ed knows.	d. They passed it. e. That is frowned upon. f. He is the one who knows.
Pronouns take the position of nouns in a sentence.	

1. In *d, They* and *it* substitute for what nouns in *a*? _____

2. In *b* and *e*, are *Cheating* and *That* subjects? _____

3. In *f*, what two pronouns take the positions that *Ed* takes in *c*? _____

_____

4. In *f*, what pronoun takes the position of *buyer* in *c*? _____

1. *boys, test*   2. *yes*   3. *He, who*   4. *one*

There are five types of pronouns:

personal:	I, you, she, he, it, they (See page 228.)
compound:	somebody else, each other, whosoever, himself
demonstrative:	this, that, these, those
relative:	who, whom, whose, that, which, what, whatever, whoever, whomever
indefinite:	all, another, any, anyone, both, each, everybody, few, many, neither, either, nobody, none, one, others, some, someone, several

Taking the position of nouns, pronouns are noun substitutes. As such, they ordinarily refer to (but do not name specifically) persons, places, animals, things, ideas, actions. A pronoun need not *mean* the same as a noun, but it must take the position that a noun takes.

> *nouns:* Wallace thinks that Mr. Lakewood is a genius.
> *pronouns: Nobody else* thinks that *he* is *one*.

A pronoun may refer to a single word (called "the antecedent") or to an idea:

Everyone should have his ticket ready. (*Everyone* is the antecedent of *his*.)
This is clear: The mayor is determined to run for reelection. (*This* refers to the idea following the colon.)

Not every pronoun has an antecedent:

> *Nobody* knows *what* tomorrow may bring.

QUICK QUIZ

Art is used as therapy in hospitals, especially mental hospitals, to help engage the interest of those who seem to have lost interest in life or to help others "get outside themselves."
　　　　　　　　　　　　　　　　　　　　　　　　—RUSSELL LYNES

1. What is the first pronoun used? What type of pronoun is it? _____

   _____

2. *Those* is the antecedent of what relative pronoun? _____

3. What indefinite pronoun is used? What compound pronoun? _____

   _____

1. *those, demonstrative*   2. *who*   3. *others, themselves*

5

SINGULAR	PLURAL
a. I changed the subject. b. This seemed reasonable. c. The one I like is red.	d. We changed the subject. e. These seemed reasonable. f. The ones I like are red.
Most pronouns indicate number by their forms.	

1. Do the pronouns in *a* and *d* show number by their forms in the same way that

   most nouns do? _____

2. Which pronoun in *f* forms its plural as a noun does? _____

1. *no*   2. *ones*

   Some pronouns are always singular: *each, either, everybody.* Other pronouns
are always plural: *several, few, both.*
   Note: A few pronouns do not indicate number by their form and may
be considered either singular or plural: *you, all, some, none, that, who, which, what.*

QUICK QUIZ

The floor of the deep ocean basins is probably as old as the sea itself. In all the
hundreds of millions of years that have intervened since the formation of the
abyss, these deeper depressions have never, as far as we can learn, been drained
of their covering waters.   —RACHEL L. CARSON

1. What is the pronoun in the first sentence? What is its number? _____

   _____

2. Does the form of the pronoun subject of *have intervened* indicate number?

   _____

3. What are the plural personal pronouns? _____

1. *itself, singular*   2. *no*   3. *we, their*

6

NOMINATIVE CASE	OBJECTIVE CASE	POSSESSIVE CASE
I, he, she, we, they, who, you, it	me, him, her, us, them, whom, you, it	my, his, her, our, your, their, whose, mine, yours, hers, ours, theirs

    a. I have a good friend who goes to Florida every winter.
    b. Aunt Dolly gave Eleanor and him an afghan.
    c. Whose course is your brother taking? His or hers?

Personal pronouns and the relative pronoun *who* change form to indicate case: nominative, objective, possessive.

1. What is the case of the pronoun subjects in *a*? _____

2. In *b*, what pronoun is in the objective case? _____

3. List the possessive pronouns in *c*. _____

4. Does any possessive pronoun above carry the apostrophe? _____

1. *nominative* 2. *him* 3. *Whose, your, His, hers* 4. *no*

    Possessive pronouns show either ownership or relationship. They function both as adjectives (see page 59) and as noun substitutes.

    ownership: The ring is Mary's. The ring is *hers*. It is *her* ring.
    relationship: He knows the value of a dollar. He knows *its* value.

The form or spelling of these pronouns indicates possessive case; they never take an apostrophe: *its, ours, theirs, yours, hers, whose*. Words like *it's, you're,* and *who's* are nominative pronouns joined to verb forms in contractions; *it is,* for example, becomes the contraction *it's*. Such indefinite pronouns as *everyone* and *another* take the apostrophe: *everyone's opinion*.

QUICK QUIZ

A. "You're tensed up again," said Mrs. Mitty. "It's one of your days."

                                               —JAMES THURBER

B. Freedom of choice lies, not in the world we see, but in our freedom to turn our eyes in this direction, or that, or to close them altogether. —W. H. AUDEN

1. In *A*, what is the possessive pronoun? _____

2. In *B*, what personal pronoun is in the nominative case? _____

3. In *B*, what personal pronoun is in the objective case? _____

1. *your* 2. *we* 3. *them*

7

NOUNS	GERUNDS
a. Win by a clever move. b. Experiments take time.	c. Win by moving cleverly. d. Reducing takes time.
Gerunds are verb forms which take the position of nouns.	

1. In *c*, what verb form takes the noun position? _____

2. What noun in *b* is replaced by a gerund in *d*? _____

3. What is the number of the gerund in *d*? _____

1. *moving* 2. *Experiments* 3. *singular*

Note: Some grammarians call the verb forms which are used as nouns or modifiers *verbals,* classifying these as gerunds, participles, and infinitives. Other grammarians define *verbal* as a word or word group which takes the verb position. In this textbook, when a verb form takes the verb position, it is classified as a *verb.* When a verb form ending in *-ing* takes the noun position, it is called a *gerund;* when a present-participle or a past-participle verb form takes the adjective position, it is labeled simply *participle.* When the infinitive verb form takes the position of a noun or a modifier, it is labeled simply *infinitive.* (See pages 230 and 251.)

> *verbs:* Katie *is sewing* for the club. Katie *will sew* all day.
> *gerund:* Katie's job is *sewing.*
> *participle:* *Sewing* for the club, Katie made twenty dollars.
> *infinitive:* Katie likes *to sew* for the club.

Gerunds do not change their form to show tense or number the way verbs do. If an *-ing* verb form takes an *s,* it is usually classified as a straight noun rather than as a gerund.

> *gerund:* *Writing* a letter is a job for me.
> *noun:* His *writings* were published posthumously.

QUICK QUIZ

A. He guessed she needed jollying.   —WILLA CATHER
B. Lyon was conscious that he was partly answered by the Colonel's not going on with the subject.   —HENRY JAMES
C. The trees were uncurling out of the darkness, and the grass was moving like a sea.   —KAY BOYLE

1. In *A*, what is the gerund? _____

2. In *B*, if the gerund phrase *not going on with the subject* were changed to the

single noun *silence,* would *Colonel's* remain possessive? _____

3. Are the -*ing* forms in *C* used as gerunds? _____

1. *jollying*   2. *yes*   3. *no*

8

NOUNS	INFINITIVES USED AS NOUNS
a. He likes the cook. b. Success is our aim. c. I did nothing except chores.	d. He likes to cook. e. To fight is futile. f. I did nothing except sleep.
Infinitives are verb forms which may take the position of nouns.	

1. In *d*, what infinitive has the position of the noun in *a*? _____

2. What is the subject of *is* in *b*? Of *is* in *e*? _____

3. In *f*, what word is understood before *sleep*? _____

4. In *f*, is the verb form *sleep* used as a noun? _____

1. *to cook*   2. *Success, To fight*   3. *to*   4. *yes*

An infinitive is a verb form which may be used as a noun, an adjective, or an adverb. An infinitive nearly always consists of the marker *to* plus the verb. When the marker is omitted, the infinitive is called a bare infinitive.

Let us try again.   I heard the man yell for help.

QUICK QUIZ

A. Gabe knew how to hunt and hold, but these things knew only how to hunt and kill.
—JAMES STREET
B. Fear made his feet fly.
—SHERWOOD ANDERSON

1. In *A*, what infinitives in the noun position have *to* understood? _____

_____

2. What is the bare infinitive in *B*? What verb does it follow? _____

1. *hold, kill*   2. *fly, made*

9

a. The fog on the highway looked like smoke. b. Into the chilly waters dived Joseph. c. There was too much talking in the laboratory. d. To race is dangerous.
Subjects of sentences are either nouns or noun substitutes.

1. In *a, what* (the subject) looked like smoke? _____

2. In *b, who* (the subject) dived? _____

3. In *c*, what gerund is used as subject of *was?* _____

4. In *d*, is *To race* used as a noun? _____

1. *fog*   2. *Joseph*   3. *talking*   4. *yes*

To find the grammatical subject of any sentence, first name the verb. Then ask *Who* (plus the verb)? Or *What* (plus the verb)? The answer is the subject, as in *1* and *2* above.

A *postponed subject* follows the verb in a sentence which begins with an expletive (*It* or *There*).

It is foolish *to worry.* (To worry is foolish.)

QUICK QUIZ

Living down there was like living in a bean pod; one could see nothing but the bed one lay in. Our horizon of woods was the limit of our world. —LAURIE LEE

1. What noun is used as a subject? _____

2. What pronoun is used twice as a subject? _____

3. What verb has a gerund for a subject? _____

1. *horizon*   2. *one*   3. *was*

10

> a. Mr. Lane may be the boss.
> b. These groceries must be yours.
> c. My favorite pastime is painting.
> d. To understand is not necessarily to forgive.
>
> **Nouns or noun substitutes may function as subject complements.**

1. In *a*, the noun *boss* complements what subject? _____

2. What sentence has an infinitive as subject complement? _____

3. What sentence has a pronoun as subject complement? _____

4. What gerund is used as a subject complement? _____

1. *Mr. Lane*   2. *d*   3. *b*   4. *painting*

A linking verb (such as forms of *be* or *become*) always connects a subject complement with its subject.

> Benedict Arnold *turned* traitor. (*was* or *became*)

The subject complement always refers to, and sometimes identifies or renames, the subject.

> That surgeon is *Dr. Dooley*. (surgeon = Dr. Dooley)
> Monkeys are not parakeets. (The linking verb *are* relates *parakeets* to *Monkeys;* the *not* qualifies the relationship.)

Sometimes a subject complement precedes the subject.

> I do not know *what* rococo is. (rococo = what)

QUICK QUIZ

A. Like the cosmos which he views, tragic man is a paradox and a mystery.
— RICHARD B. SEWALL

B. For a successful man is he who receives a great deal from his fellowmen . . . .
— ALBERT EINSTEIN

1. In A, what are the noun subject complements? _____

_____

2. In B, is *he, who,* or *fellowmen* the subject complement? _____

1. *paradox, mystery*   2. *he*

11

ONE OBJECT	TWO OBJECTS
a. Liberals forget this tenet. b. Martha wanted to help.	c. She baked us a ham. d. Hal taught them math.
Objects of verbs are either nouns or noun substitutes.	

1. In *a*, the liberals forget *what* (the object)? _____

2. In *b*, what infinitive is the object of *wanted?* _____

3. In *c*, she baked *what? For whom?* _____

4. What are the objects of *taught* in *d*? _____

1. *tenet*   2. *to help*   3. *ham, us*   4. *them, math*

Always used with action (nonlinking) verbs, objects logically answer the question *Whom?* or *What?* (or *To whom?* or *For whom?*) after the verb.

Does he have a dog?	I sent them the tickets.
question: Does he have *what?*	*questions:* Sent *what? To whom?*
object: the noun *dog*	*objects:* the noun *tickets,* the pronoun *them*

Sometimes an object precedes the verb, especially in questions and exclamations.

That I believe.   *What* did he do?   How much *weight* he's lost!

Some objects receive the action of the verb; other objects do not.

John hit the *ball*. (The ball receives the action.)
She fears only *failure*—and *mice*. I did absolutely *nothing*. (The objects receive no action.)

QUICK QUIZ

A. Old Alf kept pinching his lower lip together, and his sad brown eyes still had the rabbit-in-the-fence-corner look.   —JESSAMYN WEST
B. I, for one, have never ceased to be glad that I chose writing as my career.
                                                          —OLIVER LA FARGE

1. In A, what is the object of *kept pinching*? _____

2. Is *look*, in A, the object of a verb? _____

3. What gerund is the object of a verb in *B*? _____

1. *lip*   2. *yes*   3. *writing*

12

a. Give that to Ellen.	c. Everyone but her approved.
b. He solved many problems by marrying.	d. Lawrence has no plan except to marry.

Objects of prepositions are either nouns or noun substitutes.

1. In *a*, what noun (the object) follows the preposition *to*? _____

2. In *b*, what gerund is the object of *by*? _____

3. In *c* and *d*, what are the objects of the prepositions? _____

_____

1. *Ellen*   2. *marrying*   3. *her, to marry*

Sometimes the object of a preposition precedes the preposition, which may end the sentence. A preposition is often retained after a passive verb.

Which girl did you sit *by*? (by which girl)
The target was shot *at*. (I shot *at the target*.)

(A list of commonly used prepositions appears on page 262.)

A. We seem to have slipped into George Orwell's world of doublethink without
   knowing it.   —JEROME D. FRANK
B. What was the Maginot Line for?   —WINSTON CHURCHILL

1. In A, what two nouns are used as objects of prepositions? _____

_____

2. In A, *knowing it* is object of what preposition? _____

3. In B, what is the object of *for?* _____

1. *world, doublethink*   2. *without*   3. *What*

13

WITHOUT OBJECTS	WITH OBJECTS
a. Dick hopes to fly.	d. Dick hopes to fly a jet.
b. Asking is futile.	e. Asking him that is futile.
c. Having finished, I left.	f. Having finished counting the money, I left.

The objects (or complements) of gerunds, infinitives, and participles are generally nouns or noun substitutes.

1. In *a*, what is the infinitive? _____

2. In *d*, what noun-object answers the question *To fly what?* _____

3. In *e*, what are the two objects of the gerund? _____

4. In *f*, what gerund is object of the participle? _____

5. In *f*, what noun is object of the gerund? _____

1. *to fly*   2. *jet*   3. *him, that*   4. *counting*   5. *money*

Like the object of a verb, the object of a gerund, of an infinitive, or of a participle answers one of these questions: What? Whom? To or for what? To or for whom?

He likes to raise tulips.	Her joy is writing him love notes.
question: To raise *what?*	*questions:* Writing *what? To whom?*
object of infinitive: tulips.	*objects of gerund:* love notes, him

Sometimes the object of an infinitive comes before rather than after the infinitive.

I know *whom* to choose.   Has she decided *what* to hand in?

Although participles are verb forms used as adjectives (see page 251), they can take objects, which are nouns or noun substitutes: "I saw Dick moving heavy *furniture.*"

Note: An infinitive may have a subject, which is nearly always a noun or an objective pronoun. The subject of an infinitive answers the question *Who?* or *What?* before the infinitive.

> The officer required John to pay a fine.
> *question:*   *Who* is to pay?
> *subject of the infinitive:* John

QUICK QUIZ

A. He had a genius for making enemies.   —DEEMS TAYLOR
B. She flowed down to meet me, and we kissed formally.   —SHOW
C. To me, this is a wonderful trick, calling for a great athlete. —PAUL GALLICO

1. In A, what noun is the object of the gerund? _____

2. The objective pronoun is object of what infinitive in *B?* _____

3. What noun is the object of the participle in *C?* _____

1. *enemies* 2. *to meet* 3. *athlete*

14

```
a. I live in Oklahoma, a windy state.
b. Not a good leader, James soon resigned as foreman.
c. That job, baby-sitting, does not appeal to Larry.
d. To fail, to hate, to die—these I fear.

        Appositives are either nouns or noun substitutes.
```

1. In *a*, the appositive *state* refers to what noun? _____

2. In *b*, what noun precedes and refers to *James?* _____

3. In *c*, what gerund appositive identifies *job?* _____

4. In *d*, the three infinitives are in apposition to what pronoun? _____

1. *Oklahoma* 2. *leader* 3. *baby-sitting* 4. *these*

An appositive has reference to (may rename or identify) another noun or noun substitute in the sentence. The appositive usually follows, but may precede, the word which it is in apposition with.

Most appositives (single words or word groups) are set off by commas or dashes. Comparatively speaking, the restrictive or unpunctuated appositive (pointing out which one) is rare: "I like the poet *Keats.*"

A. Now, there are only two methods of communication for scholars, writing and speaking. —EDMUND S. MORGAN

B. Her joyless and intimidating visits had, therefore, only one object—to protect the interests of Lucille. —ELIZABETH BOWEN

C. A master of verbal ambush, he uses frontal artillery on the trite. —LEO ROSTEN

1. In A, what are the gerund appositives? What is the word they explain?

_____

2. In B, the infinitive phrase is in apposition with what noun? _____

3. In C, does the appositive phrase precede or follow the word with which it is

in apposition? _____

1. *writing, speaking, methods*   2. *object*   3. *precedes*

15

NOUNS OR PRONOUNS	PHRASES USED AS NOUNS
a. Six is too late.	d. After six o'clock is too late.
b. I like winter hikes.	e. I like going on winter hikes.
c. Jane said that.	f. Jane said to pay the milkman.
Phrases may function as nouns or noun substitutes.	

1. In d, what phrase substitutes for the subject in a? _____

_____

2. In e, what gerund phrase is used as object of the verb? _____

_____

3. In f, the infinitive phrase takes the position of what word in c? _____

_____

1. *After six o'clock*   2. *going on winter hikes*   3. *that*

Will be searching, out of the mist, me to evaluate it, and *his outwitting her* are phrases. A phrase is a group of related words which does not contain a subject-and-verb combination and which functions in the sentence as a single noun, verb, or modifier.

A phrase used as a noun takes the position of a noun in the sentence.

Eating that hard candy sent me to the dentist. (a gerund phrase taking the subject position)
Ike asked *to use the jeep.* (an infinitive phrase taking the object position)

QUICK QUIZ

A. I hate killing things.　　　　　　　　　　　　　　　　—WALLACE STEGNER
B. To read a book is to enter into contact with something alive.
　　　　　　　　　　　　　　　　　　　　　　　　　　　—CLIFTON FADIMAN
C. In his dream the man moaned but Sadao paid no heed except to mutter at him.　　　　　　　　　　　　　　　　　　　　　　　—PEARL S. BUCK

1. In A, what gerund phrase takes the noun position? _____

2. In B, do both infinitive phrases take the noun position? _____

3. In C, how is the infinitive noun phrase used? _____

_____

1. *killing things*　2. *yes*　3. *object of the preposition "except"*

16

NOUNS AND PRONOUNS	NOUN CLAUSES
a. I don't know that. b. It shocked Helen. c. After a long time, we said good-by.	d. I don't know why he is idle. e. What Don said shocked Helen. f. After what seemed forever, we said good-by.
Subordinate clauses may function as substitutes for nouns.	

1. In *d*, what word group (noun clause) substitutes for the pronoun *that* in *a*?

_____

2. In *d*, does this word group have both a subject and a verb? _____

3. In *e*, what noun clause takes the place of *It* in *b*? _____

4. Give the first and the last word of the object of the preposition in *f*. _____

_____

1. *why he is idle*　2. *yes*　3. *What Don said*　4. *what, forever*

Every clause has a subject and a verb. Every subordinate clause functions as a single noun, adjective, or adverb. A subordinate clause used as a noun is called a noun clause. It may stand anywhere in the sentence that a noun can stand and may therefore be used as a subject, an object, an appositive, and so on.

A pronoun may logically substitute for a noun clause.

PRONOUNS	NOUN CLAUSES
It is not known.	*Why he left school* is not known.
Give this to *him*.	Give this to *whoever needs it*.
Ask Mary *that*.	Ask Mary *where the leaky faucet is*.

QUICK QUIZ

He incarnated the assurances and pretenses of popular government, implied that it could and might perish from the earth. What he meant by "a new birth of freedom" for the nation could have a thousand interpretations.

—CARL SANDBURG

1. Give the first and last words of the noun clause in the first sentence. _____

_____

2. Of what verb is this noun clause the object? _____

3. Give the first and last words of the noun clause used as subject. _____

_____

1. *that, earth*   2. *implied*   3. *What, nation*

17

NOUN OR PRONOUN IN PARENTHETICAL DIRECT ADDRESS	NOUN-CENTERED PARENTHETICAL EXPRESSION
a. Mr. Chairman, I second the motion.	d. Dinner ready, Mom called out, "Soup's on!"
b. I wish you'd shave, my love.	e. They stood an hour in the rain, all cabs ignoring them.
c. Will you, little one, be quiet for a few seconds?	f. We gave up, the theater being closed, and went home.

Nouns and noun substitutes may be used in parenthetical direct address and in noun-centered expressions (nominative absolutes).

1. In *a*, who is addressed directly? _____

2. In *a* and *b*, what mark of punctuation sets off the nouns naming the ones addressed? _____

3. In *c*, is *little one* an appositive, direct address, or both? _____

4. In *d*, what is the introductory parenthetical expression? _____

_____

5. In *e* and *f*, what nouns are the center of the parenthetical expressions?

_____

A noun or noun substitute used in direct address names the person (or sometimes the thing) spoken to. Noun-centered parenthetical expressions—also called nominative absolutes—consist of a noun or a noun substitute followed by a participle, either expressed or understood. In Examples *e* and *f* above, *ignoring* and *being* are stated; in Example *d*, *being* is understood. Noun-centered parenthetical expressions as well as words of direct address are set off by commas (occasionally by dashes).

QUICK QUIZ

A. So, his arms hanging, they carried him up the steps and into the side door of the house.   —PEARL S. BUCK

B. Arms raised high, he attacked the fortissimo D flat chords of the concerto's opening.   —HARPER'S MAGAZINE

C. "There's time enough, Red Hanrahan," said the man of the house.
    —WILLIAM BUTLER YEATS

1. In *A*, what is the noun-centered parenthetical expression (nominative absolute)? _____

2. In *B*, what is the noun in the introductory parenthetical expression? What is the participle? _____

3. In *C*, what compound noun is used in direct address? _____

_____

REVIEW EXERCISE A

1. What are the three most common noun-markers? _____

2. What two endings are characteristic of the plural form of most nouns?

   _____

3. What is the plural of *son-in-law?* _____

4. Are both *somebody else* and *whosoever* compound pronouns? _____

5. Are the pronouns *either* and *everyone* always singular? _____

6. What is the possessive form of *it?* Of *who?* _____

7. Classify these pronouns as relatives or as indefinites: *one, much, all, each.*

   _____

8. In *Everybody chip in his share!* what is the antecedent of *his?* _____

   _____

9. Is every verb form ending in *-ing* a gerund? _____

10. What is generally the infinitive marker? _____

11. May both gerunds and infinitives be used as subjects and subject com-

    plements? _____

12. What type of verb does a subject complement always follow? _____

    _____

13. A direct object always follows what type of verb? _____

    _____

14. May a noun, pronoun, gerund, and infinitive all be used as objects of prepo-

    sitions? _____

15. Are there any objects in the following sentence? If so, what are they?

    Having finished counting money, I left. _____

16. Are there any subjects of infinitives in the following sentences? If so, what

are they? _____

(a) I hope to write him. _____ _____

(b) Let's go. _____

17. What two marks of punctuation may set off an appositive? _____

_____

18. May a prepositional phrase ever be used as a noun? _____

19. Does a clause always require a subject and verb? Does a phrase? _____

_____

20. What is the specific use of a noun or noun substitute which names the per-

son spoken to? _____

1. *a, an, the*   2. *-s, -es*   3. *sons-in-law*   4. *yes*   5. *yes*   6. *its, whose*   7. *indefinites*
8. *Everybody*   9. *no*   10. *to*   11. *yes*   12. *linking*   13. *action* or *nonlinking*   14. *yes*
15. *yes, counting, money*   16. *yes*   (a) *none*   (b) *us*   17. *commas and dashes*   18. *yes*
19. *yes, no*   20. *direct address*

REVIEW EXERCISE B

A. One of life's greatest tragedies is that we waste a third of it in unconsciousness.
                                                                    —HOLIDAY

   1. What three words above have endings characteristic of nouns? _____

   _____

   2. What word other than a preposition serves as a noun signal? _____

   3. What noun substitute is the subject of *is*? _____

B. She wanted to apologize for her brother-in-law's attitude.
                                                        —MORLEY CALLAGHAN

   4. If *brother-in-law's* were plural possessive, how would it be written?

   _____

   5. What is the object of *wanted*? _____

C. What do you want to stand up on a hill for?   —FORD MADOX FORD

    6. What is the object of the preposition for? _____

    7. What is the subject of the sentence? _____

D. Not to engage in this pursuit of ideas is to live like ants instead of like men.
                                             —MORTIMER J. ADLER

    8. What is the compound preposition? _____

    9. Write the first and last words of the complete phrase subject of the sen-

       tence. _____

   10. Write the first and last words of the complete phrase subject complement.

       _____

E. It was I who banged the table now, without any of the reserve of decency.
                                           —WILBUR DANIEL STEELE

  11. What is the subject complement? _____

  12. What is the relative pronoun? _____

  13. What is the indefinite pronoun? _____

F. Consider the theatre, that faithful mirror of a society's preoccupations.
                                         —ARTHUR SCHLESINGER, JR.

  14. What is the key noun in the appositive phrase? _____

  15. If *a* were changed to *the* and if *society* were made plural, how would the

      latter be written? _____

G. It is difficult to know what to do, whom to fight, where to look for allies.
                                         —IRWIN SHAW

  16. Give the first and last words of the postponed subject._____

  17. What is the complement of the infinitive *to do?* _____

      Of *to fight?* _____

  18. The last three infinitives are objects of what? _____

H. I learned to read before I was four years old, my reading then consisting of the fairy tales of the Brothers Grimm and Hans Andersen. —EDITH SITWELL

19. What is the gerund in this sentence? _____

20. Write the first and last words of the noun-centered parenthetical phrase.

_____

I. The sheriff had his back to the crowd and he was saying something to Jim. Jim did not hear what he said. —ERSKINE CALDWELL

21. What is the antecedent of *he* and *his*? _____

22. What are the first and last words of the noun clause used as a direct

object? _____

J. You must act, man, or you are lost. —A. CONAN DOYLE

23. What is the noun used in direct address? _____

K. He was more than annoyed, he was disgusted, to find that half the people on board were talking English. —ALFRED NOYES

24. Give the first and last words of the noun clause used as complement of

the infinitive. _____

25. What noun has no singular form? _____

1. *life's, tragedies, unconsciousness* 2. *a* 3. *one* 4. *brothers-in-law's* 5. *to apologize*
6. *What* 7. *you* 8. *instead of* 9. *Not...ideas* 10. *to...men* 11. *I* 12. *who* 13. *any*
14. *mirror* 15. *societies'* 16. *to...allies* 17. *what, whom* 18. *to know* 19. *reading*
20. *my...Andersen* 21. *sheriff* 22. *what...said* 23. *man* 24. *that...English* 25. *people*

modifiers 3

1

WORDS NOT MODIFIED	WORDS MODIFIED
a. They are Americans. b. Eyelids blinked. c. There lies Mopsy.	d. They are not loyal Americans. e. Eyelids blinked in holy horror. f. There lies Mopsy, indescribably dead.
Modifiers qualify other words or word groups.	

1. What are the modifiers in *d*? _____

2. What qualifier in *e* changes the meaning of *b*? _____

3. What word in *f* really makes a difference in Mopsy's condition? _____

4. What word in *f* gives added force by qualifying the modifier *dead*? _____

_____

1. *not loyal*   2. *in holy horror*   3. *dead*   4. *indescribably*

The noun markers *a, an,* and *the* (the "articles") are the most frequently used modifiers in the language.

Possessive nouns and pronouns function as modifiers:

my idea, Frank's typewriter, no concern of yours

QUICK QUIZ

A fire engine, out for a trial spin, roared past Emerson's house, hot with readiness for public duty.   —E. B. WHITE

1. What does *hot* modify? _____

2. What possessive noun is used as a modifier? _____

3. What does the phrase *with readiness* modify? _____

1. *fire engine*   2. *Emerson's*   3. *hot*

SINGLE-WORD MODIFIERS	PHRASE MODIFIERS
a. It is a questionable statement. b. He always yawns.	c. It is a statement to be questioned. d. He yawns in class.
CLAUSE MODIFIERS	
e. It is a statement that the reporters question. f. He yawns when his guests overstay.	
A modifier may be a single word, a phrase, or a clause.	

1. In *c*, what noun is modified? In *a*? _____

2. Name the modifiers in *b* and in *d*. _____

3. In *e*, what noun is modified by a clause? _____

4. What does the clause modify in *f*? _____

1. *statement* 2. *always, in class* 3. *statement* 4. *yawns*

The importance of qualifiers in communicating ideas is illustrated by the following sentences, in which modifiers (italicized) account for over two-thirds of the words used:

> *The* water rose *farther* and dressed *Simon's coarse* hair *with brightness. The* line *of his cheek* silvered and *the* turn *of his shoulder* became *sculptured* marble. *The strange attendant* creatures, *with their fiery eyes and trailing vapors,* busied themselves *round his head.* —WILLIAM GOLDING

Modern English tends to stack up modifiers (italicized below) before the word modified:

> *Such highly trained* investigators include not only *former military and Central Intelligence Agency* specialists . . . but graduates of *such other intelligence* agencies as *the . . . former General Accounting Office* watchdogs. —VANCE PACKARD

QUICK QUIZ

All her gestures were liquid and possessed of an inner rhythm that flowed to inevitable completion with the finality of architecture or music. —AGNES DE MILLE

1. What single word modifies *completion?* _____

2. What does the phrase *of architecture or music* modify? _____

3. What are the first and last words of the modifying clause? _____

1. *inevitable* 2. *finality* 3. *that . . . music*

3

NOUNS OR NOUN SUBSTITUTES WITHOUT MODIFIERS	NOUNS OR NOUN SUBSTITUTES WITH MODIFIERS
a. He loves me. b. The leaves turned. c. Bridging gaps is a task. d. Dr. Fitz has retired because of illness.	e. Only he loves me. f. The leaves turned scarlet. g. She managed a clever bridging of gaps. h. Dr. Fitz, who is ill, has retired.
Adjectives modify nouns or noun substitutes.	

1. In *e*, what modifies the subject-pronoun *he?* _____

2. In *f*, what does *scarlet* modify? _____

3. In *c*, what is the subject? _____

4. In *g*, what words are modifiers of the gerund phrase? _____

5. In *h*, what does the parenthetical clause modify? _____

1. *only* 2. *leaves* 3. *Bridging gaps* 4. *a clever* 5. *Dr. Fitz*

Such endings as *-able, -al, -en, -ic, -ish, -less, -like, -ly, -ous,* and *-y* characterize single-word adjectives:

comfortable, mannish, hopeless, womanly, athletic

Adjectives have a relatively fixed word order: near words modified, near linking verbs, at the end of a sentence.

> *These* letters may be *important.*
> He made the alley *attractive.*
> *Frightened,* Rusty lay on the ground, *silent* and *alert.*

Words commonly used as nouns, pronouns, prepositions, or even verbs (column 1 below) may shift function and serve as adjectives (column 2).

That outfit is for *Easter.*	That is my *Easter* outfit.
Those are ripe.	*Those* plums are ripe.
He jumped *over* the fence.	The game was *over.*
Those trucks *dump* gravel.	Those are *dump* trucks.

QUICK QUIZ

A. This time Guiseppe was very careful to keep his face grave. —JOHN HERSEY
B. He stood frozen in his tracks, afraid to move. —JESSE STUART

1. In *A*, what characteristic ending does the adjective subject complement have?

2. In *A*, what does *grave* modify? _____

3. In *B*, is *frozen* a verb or a subject complement? _____

4. In *B*, what does *afraid* modify? _____

1. *-ful* 2. *face* 3. *subject complement* 4. *He*

4

a. Insecure men brag.	d. Some men almost never brag.
b. Some men never brag.	e. He likes to brag loudly.
c. Rather insecure, some men brag.	f. Finally, some men brag.

Adverbs modify words which are *not* nouns or pronouns.

1. In *b*, what adverb modifies *brag?* _____

2. In *c*, what adverb modifies what adjective? _____

3. In *d*, what adverb modifies another adverb? _____

4. In *e*, does *loudly* modify *likes* or *to brag* or both? _____

5. In *f*, what adverb modifies the rest of the sentence? _____

1. *never* 2. *Rather, insecure* 3. *almost* 4. *to brag* 5. *Finally*

Although words such as *early* and *daily* may be either an adjective or an adverb, the *-ly* added to a noun forms an adjective, and the *-ly* added to an adjective forms an adverb.

> *Adjectives ending in -ly:* friendly, manly
> *Adverbs ending in -ly:*   commonly, patiently

A word commonly used as a noun, pronoun, preposition, or adjective (column 1 below) may shift function and serve as an adverb (column 2).

> *Christmas* is tomorrow.   I am *Christmas* shopping now.
> *That* is stupid.   He couldn't be *that* stupid.
> Go *down* the steps.   Go *down*.
> They are *pretty*.   They are *pretty* dumb.

Some word groups may act as adverb equivalents.

> I knew that *right off!* (immediately)
> That is *next to* impossible. (almost)

Adverbs modifying verbs or the rest of the sentence generally have a less fixed word order than adjectives.

> *Honestly*, Kate sometimes lies.
> Kate, *honestly*, sometimes lies.
> Kate sometimes lies—*honestly!*

A. Then mother came serenely waddling in. —RUTH SUCKOW
B. As a rule, you can best study it in private conversations. —GEORGE ORWELL

1. In *A*, what are the three adverbs? _____

2. In *B*, are both prepositional phrases used as adverbs? _____

3. In *B*, is *best* an adjective or an adverb? _____

1. *Then, serenely, in* 2. *yes* 3. *adverb*

5

POSITIVE	COMPARATIVE	SUPERLATIVE
a. Fred is kind.	Chet is kinder.	Tod is kindest of all.
b. He often obeys.	I obey more often.	She obeys most often.
Many adjectives and adverbs indicate degrees of comparison.		

1. In *a*, what two endings form the comparative and superlative of the adjective?

_____

2. In *b*, what is the comparative of *often?* _____

3. In *b*, which word indicates the superlative? _____

1. *-er, -est* 2. *more often* 3. *most*

The regular comparison of one-syllable words takes -*er* and -*est*. These endings are used for two-syllable words when they do not make for awkwardness: *simple, simpler, simplest*. The regular comparison of words with three or more syllables, and of some words with two syllables, takes *more, most, less, least: harmful, less harmful, least harmful*.

A few modifiers have irregular comparison forms—such as *bad, worse, worst* and *good, better, best*.

Separated by a comma, such correlative comparatives as the following may stand together as a sentence.

The sooner, the better.   The more, the merrier.

QUICK QUIZ

A. It was only through the severest self-discipline that Washington attained his characteristic pose and serenity. —SAMUEL ELIOT MORISON
B. It is easier to love humanity as a whole than to love one's neighbor.

  —ERIC HOFFER

1. In *A*, which modifier has the superlative form? _____

2. In *A* and *B*, are the comparisons of the modifiers regular or irregular? _____

_____

3. In *B*, what ending is used for the two-syllable modifier? _____

1. *severest* 2. *regular* 3. *-er*

6

ADJECTIVE PHRASES	ADVERB PHRASES
a. He loves the girl in the red dress. b. The situation is without hope.	c. He kissed the girl on the cheek. d. Lonely without Peggy, he took a stroll.
Nearly all prepositional phrases function as modifiers.	

1. In *a* and *c*, what words do the prepositional phrases modify? _____

_____

2. In *b*, what is the phrase equivalent for *hopeless?* _____

3. In *d*, what adjective does the phrase modify? _____

1. *girl, kissed* 2. *without hope* 3. *Lonely*

 The adjective phrase nearly always follows the noun or pronoun modified. If it precedes the word modified, the adjective phrase is usually hyphenated. (See page 253.)

 The adverb phrase qualifying another modifier also has a fixed position near the word modified. The adverb phrase qualifying a verb or the rest of the sentence, however, is more mobile, frequently found at the beginning or at the end of the sentence.

> Beautiful at night, fireworks delighted the crowds. (*At night* is near *beautiful*, the word modified.)
> We had a test on Friday. On Friday we had a test. (*On Friday* is a mobile adverb phrase.)

QUICK QUIZ

A dweller in the Sahara, unfamiliar with mountains or beaches, could hardly have conceived of ski jumping and surf riding.   —ARTHUR C. CLARKE

1. What noun does the first prepositional phrase modify? _____

2. What prepositional phrase modifies an adjective? _____

_____

1. *dweller*   2. *with mountains or beaches*

7

PARTICIPIAL PHRASES	INFINITIVE PHRASES
a. Awakened at five, Larry was cross.	c. We stopped to buy a cold watermelon.
b. I heard him sneaking up the back steps.	d. I had absolutely no news to tell him.
Participial phrases function as adjectives; infinitive phrases may function as adjectives or adverbs (or as nouns).	

1. What words do the participles in *a* and *b* modify? _____

2. In *c* and *d*, what words do the infinitive phrases modify? _____

_____

3. Which infinitive phrase functions as an adjective? _____

1. *Larry, him*   2. *stopped, news*   3. *to tell him*

Participles and participial phrases are always used as adjectives. Like other adjectives, participial phrases are usually placed near the words they modify. Infinitive phrases modifying a verb or the rest of a clause or sentence often tell *why* —the *to* marker means *in order to.* Other infinitive modifiers may be implicit passives.

> We left early to avoid the five o'clock rush. (*in order to avoid*—infinitive used as adverb)
> The place to avoid is the workroom. (the place *to be avoided*—implicit passive infinitive used as adjective modifying *place*)

Note: Occasionally -*ing* verb forms may be used as adverbs. In the following sentence, *scalding* is an adverb modifying the adjective *hot: The tea is scalding hot.*

QUICK QUIZ

A. To correct one abuse we were ready to upset many a benefit.
                                                    —THORNTON WILDER

B. One day, perhaps, the earth will have been turned into one vast feather bed, with man's body dozing on top of it and his mind underneath, like Desdemona, smothered.
                                                    —ALDOUS HUXLEY

1. Are the infinitive phrases in *A* used as adjectives, adverbs, or nouns? _____

_____

2. In *B*, what does the participial phrase beginning with *dozing* modify? _____

_____

1. *adverbs* 2. *body*

8

SINGLE-WORD MODIFIERS	CLAUSE MODIFIERS
a. I need a good watch.	d. I need a watch that keeps good time.
b. Margaret will read *Walden* next.	e. Margaret will read *Walden* when she has time.
c. That was a farewell glance.	f. That was a you-go-your-way-and-I'll-go-mine glance.
Clauses may function as adjectives or as adverbs.	

1. In *d*, what adjective clause is a substitute for *good* in *a*? _____

2. What word introduces the adverb clause in *e*? _____

3. In *f*, does the hyphenated compound clause function as an adjective or as an

adverb? _____

1. *that keeps good time* 2. *when* 3. *adjective*

Adjective clauses nearly always follow the noun or noun substitute modified. The adjective clause is hyphenated when it precedes the word modified. Introductory words such as *who, whom, whose, that, which* are sometimes omitted before an adjective (and a noun) clause.

> The girl I love is beside me. (*whom* I love)

Adverb clauses generally begin with such subordinating relaters as *after, although, because, before, if, since, than, when, where,* and *while.* (See page 266.) An adverb clause may be elliptical; that is, it may have words understood rather than stated.

> Herman peels apples faster than I. (. . . than I *do*.)
> When shaving, Dad doesn't answer me. (When *he is* . . .)

QUICK QUIZ

There was once an American who said that the only important thing in life was "to set a chime of words ringing in a few fastidious minds." As far as can be learned, he left this country in a huff to tinkle his little bell in a foreign land.

—ALAN SIMPSON

1. What does the adjective clause modify? _____

2. What is the first word of the adverb clause? _____

1. *American*   2. *as*

9

UNHYPHENATED MODIFIERS	HYPHENATED MODIFIERS
a. carpeting from wall to wall b. a boy ten years old c. machine that picks cotton	d. wall-to-wall carpeting e. a ten-year-old boy f. cotton-picking machine
When placed before the word modified, word groups functioning as a single adjective are hyphenated.	

1. What preposition used in *a* is dropped in the hyphenated modifier in *d*?____

   _____

2. In *e*, what letter used in *b* is dropped? _____

3. (a) Does the verb form in *c* change when hyphenated in *f*? _____

   (b) Does the position of *cotton* change? _____

1. *from*   2. *-s*   3. *yes, yes*

The popularity of hyphenated modifiers is increasing, as the list of the modifiers below shows. All of them appeared on a single page, selected at random from *Harper's Magazine*.

an unheard-of notion	in the middle-income housing
a four-room apartment	in Lapidus-designed buildings
floor-to-ceiling doors	check-in and check-out procedures
a straight-line façade	well-known psychological differences

QUICK QUIZ

A. The damp-stone smell of the books was all he needed.

—THE ATLANTIC MONTHLY

B. The house is surrounded by three well-kept irrigated acres.

—THE ATLANTIC MONTHLY

C. The schedule of classes seems to be fast approaching a we-never-close basis.

—THE ATLANTIC MONTHLY

1. In A, what word does *damp-stone* modify? _____

2. In *B*, how many word units modify *acres?* _____

What word does *well* modify? _____

3. In *C*, is the hyphenated qualifier a phrase or a clause? _____

1. *smell*   2. *three, kept*   3. *clause*

10

a. Dickens's penname, incidentally, was Boz.
b. I know his father, who dives for pearls.
c. Chosen as an All-American, Steve is our campus hero.
d. Another classic, so they say, is *Pilgrim's Progress*.
Single words and word groups may be parenthetical modifiers.

1. In *a*, what punctuation sets off the adverb? _____

2. In *b*, is the parenthetical clause used as an adjective or as an adverb? _____

_____

3. In *c*, what past participle heads the parenthetical phrase? _____

4. In *d*, what clause is used parenthetically? _____

1. *commas*   2. *adjective*   3. *Chosen*   4. *so they say*

Whether they are single words, phrases, or clauses, parenthetical adverbs modifying the rest of the sentence have mobility: they can introduce, interrupt, or end a sentence. The tag or boomerang question, however, has a fixed position at the end of the sentence: "Long Island is ninety miles long, *isn't it?*"

A parenthetical adjective clause or phrase does not identify or restrict the meaning of the word it modifies. The voice distinguishes these modifiers by a lowering of pitch and by a pause both before and after the parenthetical element.

not parenthetical:	Those boys who played fair won the game.
voice pattern:	Those boys who played fair ‖ won the game.
parenthetical:	Those boys, who played fair, won the game.
voice pattern:	Those boys ‖ won the game.
	who played fair

Some parenthetical word groups are introduced by *not*.

I ate too much pie, not to mention the turkey.
It is Burton, not his twin, whom I know well.

Such word groups as *of course, on the other hand, I know,* and *that is to say* are often used as parenthetical transitional expressions or qualifiers.

Most of the time, commas set off parenthetical elements; however, dashes or parentheses may replace the commas.

QUICK QUIZ

A. Maybe these professors, whom I greatly respected, did not know it all.
                                                                —LINCOLN STEFFENS

B. As I went in, the first person I saw, sitting on the right hand of the Master, was Rutherford himself.   —C. P. SNOW

1. In A, would the parenthetical adjective clause make sense in any other position in the sentence? _____

2. In B, what are the first and last words of the parenthetical clause? _____

_____

3. In B, what are the first and last words of the parenthetical phrase? _____

_____

1. *no* 2. *As ... in* 3. *sitting ... Master*

REVIEW EXERCISE A

1. A modifier may be a single word, a phrase, or a _____

2. What type of modifier qualifies a noun? _____

3. Do the endings *-able, -ish, -like, -y* characterize an adjective or an adverb?

    _____

4. How can the prepositional phrase *without hope* be converted to a single-word

    adjective? _____

5. Is *-ly* a suffix used only for adverbs? _____

6. May *comfortable* be used correctly as an adverb? _____

7. Do adjectives have a relatively fixed word order? _____

8. What type of modifier does *not* modify a noun or a pronoun? _____

    _____

9. What suffixes generally show comparison? _____

10. Adjectives used as subject complements follow what type of verb? _____

    _____

11. Give the function of the prepositional phrase in this sentence: *Hal jumped*

    into the water. _____

12. How is the prepositional phrase *on the table* used in *Did Jude borrow*

    the cups on the table? _____

13. Does a participle or a gerund always function as an adjective? _____

    _____

14. How is the *-ing* verb form used in *The wind is freezing cold?* _____

15. In speech, how are parenthetical modifiers indicated? _____

    _____

16. In writing, how are parenthetical modifiers set off? _____

    _____

17. Give the function of the first infinitive phrase in *The thing to do is to take a*

    break. _____

18. Give the function of the infinitive phrase in *I often lie down to take a nap.*

    _____

19. Is *bad* an adjective or an adverb? _____

20. Is the italicized clause below used as an adjective or as an adverb? _____
    Now that we have seen the Civil Defense film, we are more prepared to cope with
    the dangers of radioactive dust.

1. *clause* 2. *adjective* 3. *adjective* 4. *using -less: hopeless* 5. *no* 6. *no* 7. *yes* 8. *adverb*
9. *-er, -est* 10. *linking* 11. *adverb* 12. *adjective* 13. *participle* 14. *adverb* 15. *pauses and lower pitch* 16. *by commas, dashes,* or *parentheses* 17. *adjective* 18. *adverb* 19. *adjective*
20. *adverb*

REVIEW EXERCISE B

A. Perhaps table manners are not a bad test of sincerity.   —GEORGE ORWELL

    1. Is *Perhaps* an adjective or an adverb? _____

    2. What is the single-word adjective? _____

    3. What word does *of sincerity* modify? _____

B. Even when people play as badly as I do, they should continue: It will help
   them to listen.   —E. M. FORSTER

    4. What adverb falls between *as* and *as?* _____

    5. What word does *badly* modify? _____

    6. What words signal the two adverb clauses? _____

C. Even more important than the living presence of a great idea is its future.
                                                      —MORTIMER J. ADLER

    7. What adjective is a subject complement? _____

8. What modifier indicates comparison? _____

9. What word is both a pronoun and an adjective? _____

D. It is a book I had to grow up to.   —CLIFTON FADIMAN

   10. What is object of the preposition *to?* _____

   11. What does the prepositional phrase modify? _____

   12. What does the clause modify? _____

E. In fact, like each and all of us, he is more or less the slave of historical relativity.   —ARNOLD TOYNBEE

   13. What is the adverb equivalent meaning *practically* or *virtually?* _____

_____

   14. What prepositional phrase modifies two pronouns, themselves objects of

     a preposition? _____

F. The first man to reach it jerked the six-foot crowbar out of the soft earth where it had been jabbed.   —ERSKINE CALDWELL

   15. What word does the infinitive phrase modify? _____

   16. What word does the prepositional phrase modify? _____

   17. What are the first and last words of the clause used as a modifier? _____

_____

G. The least a man can do at such a time is to declare himself and tell where he stands.   —E. B. WHITE

   18. What word does the clause used as a modifier qualify? _____

H. He stood on the very sill of the door, as if refusing to enter until he was perfectly sure of his rights.   —LIONEL TRILLING

   19. What word does *very* modify? Is *very* an adjective or an adverb? _____

_____

   20. What two words introduce the elliptical adverb clause? _____

1. *adverb* 2. *bad* 3. *test* 4. *badly* 5. *play* 6. *when, as* 7. *important* 8. *more* 9. *its*
10. *that* or *which* 11. *grow up* 12. *book* 13. *more or less* 14. *of us* 15. *man* 16. *jerked*
17. *where . . . jabbed* 18. *least* 19. *sill, adjective* 20. *as if*

relaters and expletives 4

1

UNRELATED		RELATED
a. the man	the train	b. the man on the train
		c. the man under the train
d. I decided.	Tom was on	e. I decided that Tom was on vacation.
vacation.		f. I decided when Tom was on vacation.

Relaters connect single words, phrases, or clauses and show the relationships between them.

1. In *b* and *c*, what two words relate the words in *a*? _____

2. In *e* and *f*, what two words relate the ideas in *d*? _____

1. *on, under*   2. *that, when*

Relaters do not make an assertion (as verbs do) and do not qualify (as modifiers do); relaters are connectives. Relaters need not be placed between the words or the word groups related.

> *When* Tom was on vacation, I decided.
> What did Jeanette open that box *for?*

QUICK QUIZ

He looked shyly about the lighted hall, seeking a confusion of strange faces, the people moving down the aisles to seats, and he was excited and expectant.
— JAMES FARRELL

1. What word relates *the lighted hall* to *looked shyly?* _____

2. *Excited* is linked to *expectant* by what relater? _____

3. Does the first *and* relate single words or phrases or clauses? _____

1. *about*   2. *and*   3. *clauses*

2

> a. Please repair the steps at the back.
> b. To whom did you send the lamp? Whom did you send it to?
> c. Find the box that the lamp came in.
> d. A man in rags today may, of course, be the owner of oil wells tomorrow, according to Peter.

A preposition relates its object to another word or word group.

1. In *a*, *back* is the object of what preposition? _____

2. In *b*, what is the object of *to* in both sentences? _____

3. In *c*, *that* is the object of what preposition? _____

4. How many prepositional phrases are there in *d*? _____

1. *at* 2. *whom* 3. *in* 4. *four*

A preposition ordinarily precedes, but sometimes follows its object: *What did he stand on?* The object of a preposition may also serve as a connective. The object may be understood rather than stated.

> He is a person whom you should vote for.
> He is a person you should vote for.

In these sentences, *whom* is not only the object of *for* but also a connective linking the adjective clause to the word modified, *person.*

Such words as *up, out, in,* and *on* may be used as prepositions, as parts of the verb, or as adverbs. Meaning, not position, determines the classification of the word.

> *preposition:* He turned up Main Street.
> *part of the verb:* He turned up before lunch, and he turned up sober.
> *adverb:* She turned up the hem. She turned the hem up.

The following words are often used as prepositions:

about	before	for	on account of
according to	behind	from	out
across	below	in (into)	over
after	beneath	in order to	since
against	beside (besides)	in spite of	through
along	between	instead of	to (toward)
among	by	like	under
around	down	of	until
as to	during	off	up (upon)
at	except	on	with (without)
because of			

Prepositions may be used in groups. "The cat ran *out from under* the car."

QUICK QUIZ

As the hero's horse tires, Hurricane Nell seizes the man about the waist, raises him high overhead "by the power of her wonderful arms," and deposits him on the back of the wild stallion. —HENRY NASH SMITH

1. Within the quotation marks, *of* relates *arms* to what noun? _____

2. The second *of* relates *back* to what noun? _____

3. What are the other prepositions? _____

1. *power*   2. *stallion*   3. *about, by, on*

3

> a. Mozart's Italian operas are the ones that I prefer.
> b. *Nowhither*, which is not archaic, means "toward no definite place."
> c. Jack joined the group whose purpose is to develop civic leaders.
>
> **Relative pronouns function as relaters in subordinate clauses.**

1. In *a*, the relative pronoun *that* links the adjective clause to what other word

in the sentence? _____

2. In *b*, what is the pronoun relater? _____

3. In *c*, does *whose* relate a phrase or a clause to the noun *group?* _____

1. *ones*   2. *which*   3. *clause*

   Relative pronouns—*who (whom, whose), which, that, what, whoever, whomever, whosever, whichever, whatever*—are both pronouns and connectives.

> These are the men who succeed. (*Who* is subject of *succeed* and relates the adjective clause to *men*.)
> George is the one for whom we staged a ticker-tape parade. (*Whom* is object of *for* and relates the clause to *one*.)

QUICK QUIZ

The lunatic who thinks he is a crowned head may be, in a sense, happy, but his happiness is not of a kind that any sane person would envy. —BERTRAND RUSSELL

1. What relaters introduce adjective clauses? _____

2. Which of these relaters is a subject as well as a connective? _____

3. Which of these relaters is an object? _____

1. *who, that*   2. *who*   3. *that*

4

WITHOUT RELATERS	WITH RELATERS
a. green yellow b. what you say what you think c. The rain diminished. The flood receded.	d. green or yellow e. not only what you say but also what you think f. As the rain diminished, the flood receded.
Conjunctions connect and relate single words, phrases, clauses.	

1. In *d*, what relater connects items in *a*? _____

2. In *e*, what relaters are added to items in *b*? _____

_____

3. In *f*, what conjunction relates the clauses? _____

1. *or*   2. *not only, but also*   3. *as*

Unlike a preposition, which must be part of a prepositional phrase, a conjunction is not a marker of a noun and never takes an object.

Words such as *but, for, since,* and *before* may function either as prepositions or as conjunctions.

> *prepositions:* I saw everyone there *but* Grandma.
> Felton was served *before* me.
> *conjunctions:* I saw everyone there, *but* Grandma didn't.
> Felton was served *before* I was.

QUICK QUIZ

A. I used to take my bicycle and ride out into the country, but the country was strange, too, and ugly to my eyes, all flat and dull.   —VICTORIA LINCOLN

B. As we watched, the buzzards, careening and narrowing their circles, began to descend.   —WILLIAM ALEXANDER PERCY

1. In A, what relater connects verbs in the first clause? _____

2. Is *but* a preposition or a conjunction? _____

3. What relaters connect adjectives? _____

4. In B, what are the two conjunctions? _____

1. *and*   2. *conjunction*   3. *and*   4. *As, and*

5

COORDINATE STRUCTURES	COORDINATING CONJUNCTIONS
a. angles, curves b. in school, out of school c. how the novel begins, how it ends	d. angles or curves e. in school and out of school f. neither how the novel begins nor how it ends

Coordinating conjunctions connect and relate single words, phrases, and clauses of the same grammatical construction.

1. What in *d* relates the single words? _____

2. What in *e* relates the prepositional phrases? _____

3. What two coordinators connect and relate the clauses in *f*? _____

_____

1. *or*   2. *and*   3. *neither, nor*

The coordinating conjunctions *and, or, but, nor* connect single words, phrases, and clauses. However, *for, so,* and *yet,* when used as conjunctions, join and relate only main or independent clauses. Some conjunctions (correlative conjunctions) are used in pairs:

both . . . and	not . . . but	neither . . . nor
as . . . as	not only . . . but	either . . . or
not so . . . as	not only . . . but also	whether . . . or

As a transitional device, a coordinating conjunction may begin a sentence and thus relate that sentence to the preceding sentence.

QUICK QUIZ

A. The wires sagged somewhat beneath this load, but sooner or later the very weight of the snow overcame its cohesive power.   —GEORGE R. STEWART

B. When land is given, both the donor and the receiver are changed.

—ARTHUR KOESTLER

1. In A, which conjunction relates two adverbs? Which relates two clauses?

_____

2. In B, what are the correlative conjunctions? _____

1. *or, but*   2. *both, and*

6

SIMPLE SENTENCES	COMPLEX SENTENCES
a. He is honest. You know it.	c. You know that he is honest.
b. A honey mouse is a plant. A honey eater is a bird.	d. Whether or not a honey mouse is a plant, a honey eater is a bird.

A subordinating conjunction not only introduces a clause and forces it to be subordinate but also relates it to a main clause.

1. In *c*, what conjunction makes a subordinate clause out of the first sentence in

a? _____

2. In *d*, what words force the first sentence in *b* to be subordinate? _____

_____

1. *that*   2. *Whether or not*

8

SENTENCES WITHOUT EXPLETIVES	SENTENCES WITH EXPLETIVES
a. Nothing is here. b. Worrying helps!	c. There is nothing here. d. It helps to worry!
Expletives are stopgaps for postponed subjects.	

1. In *c*, what is the postponed subject of *is?* _____

2. In *c*, what word (expletive) takes the subject position? _____

3. In *d*, what is the postponed subject? _____

4. In *d*, what is the expletive? _____

1. *nothing* 2. *There* 3. *to worry* 4. *It*

There and *it* are very frequently used as expletives or fillers without meaning; they start a sentence or a clause by taking the subject position (before the verb).

It may serve either as a pronoun or an expletive; *there* may function as an adverb, a noun, an interjection, or as an expletive.

nonexpletives: *It* exploded. (*It*, a pronoun, is the subject.)
　　　　　　　There he goes! (*There* is an adverb.)
expletives:　　*It* is true the ship exploded. (That the ship exploded is true.)
　　　　　　　There was nobody in the hall. (Nobody was in the hall.)

As expletives, *there* and *it* differ in one important respect: *it* is invariably considered singular (*it is, it has,* and so on), but *there* may be followed by *is* or *are, was* or *were,* and so on—the choice of verb form depending upon the postponed subject.

QUICK QUIZ

A. There is a paradox here. Language lives; it lasts longer than any human life.
—GILBERT HIGHET

B. It is certainly striking that there is not a trace of gradual development in the high civilizations which once stretched from Mexico to Peru.
—THOR HEYERDAHL

1. In *A*, what is the expletive? _____

2. In *A*, what is the postponed subject? _____

3. In *B*, is *it* a pronoun or an expletive? _____

4. In *B*, is *there* an expletive or an adverb? _____

1. *There* 2. *paradox* 3. *expletive* 4. *expletive*

REVIEW EXERCISE A

1. In "the girl at the office," what is the relater? _____

2. In "often injured while playing," what is the relater? _____

3. Must a preposition be part of a phrase? _____

4. Does a preposition ordinarily follow its object? _____

5. May *who, which, what,* and *that* all function as relative pronouns? _____

6. Do relative pronouns often introduce subordinate clauses? _____

7. Must a conjunction be part of a phrase? _____

8. May a conjunction be part of a phrase? _____

9. Do coordinating conjunctions relate words and word groups of like or of unlike construction? _____

10. What companion relater is often used with *nor?* _____

11. Does a subordinating conjunction force a clause to be subordinate? _____

12. May *after, as, whether,* and *once* all act as subordinating conjunctions?

_____

13. What mark of punctuation usually follows an introductory adverb clause?

_____

14. What mark of punctuation precedes an adverbial conjunction placed between two main clauses? _____

15. Does *for* function only as a preposition? Does *but?* _____

16. In simple sentences beginning with an expletive, what is the usual sentence pattern? _____

17. Expletives are stopgaps for what? _____

_____

18. May an expletive follow a verb? _____

19. May the expletive *there* be followed by *are?* _____

20. Write the expletive in this sentence: *It was snowing, and there were no cabs*

    available. _____

REVIEW EXERCISE B

A. The young man cleared his throat, without necessity or success, producing a
   small, syncopated noise.   —DOROTHY PARKER

   1. What are the two relaters? _____

   2. Which is the conjunction? Which is the preposition? _____

   _____

B. With his hand, he shielded his eyes for a moment against the harsh, watty glare
   from the naked bulb over the table.   —J. D. SALINGER

   3. What is the first relater in the sentence? _____

   4. What word relates *glare* to *shielded?* _____

   5. What word relates *table* and *bulb?* _____

C. There is something to be said for a bad education.   —PHYLLIS MC GINLEY

   6. What is the expletive? _____

   7. What is the prepositional relater? _____

D. Though such an indifferent painter, he had been a Michelangelo of friendship.
                                                     —THE NEW YORKER

   8. What is the subordinating conjunction? _____

   9. What is the preposition? _____

   10. What words are understood in the elliptical clause? _____

E. His children were not only numerous but physically large, and this physical largeness prevails to the present day. —JOHN J. CONSIDINE

11. What paired conjunctions are used? _____

12. What coordinating conjunction is used to relate main clauses? _____

F. I am sure that he was unconscious of any connection between these widely separated statements; but it was certainly there. —ROBERT SHERWOOD

13. What is the subordinating conjunction? _____

14. What is the subject of the second *was?* _____

15. What adverbs, if any, are used in the second main clause? _____

_____

G. It is true that age cannot wither her nor custom stale her infinite variety. Nevertheless, the American woman is under attack. —M. F. ASHLEY MONTAGU

16. What relater introduces the subject? _____

17. What is the expletive? _____

18. What is the coordinating conjunction? the adverbial conjunction? _____

_____

H. Now and then the raft disappeared completely behind the black seas; then she rose again and stood out sharp in silhouette against the stars, while glittering water poured from the logs. —THOR HEYERDAHL

19. What adverbial conjunction links the main clauses? _____

20. What relater introduces the subordinate clause? _____

1. *without, or* 2. *or, without* 3. *with* 4. *against* 5. *over* 6. *There* 7. *for* 8. *Though*
9. *of* 10. *he was* 11. *not only, but* 12. *and* 13. *that* 14. *it* 15. *certainly, there* 16. *that*
17. *It* 18. *nor, Nevertheless* 19. *then* 20. *while*

index

a

a, an, the as noun markers, 223
absolute phrase, 238, *Patterns 139, 140*
action verb, 87, 232–33
active voice, 29, 214, *Pattern 177*
address, direct, 238–39
adjective: defined, 247; distinguished from adverbs, 87, 248; forms of comparison, 87, 249; position, 87, 213, 247; suffixes, 247, *Exercises 89–91, 95, 99–102, Patterns 105–07*
adjective clause, 246, 252, 254, *Patterns 113, 132*
adjective phrase, 250
adverb: defined, 248; distinguished from adjective, 87, 248; equivalents, 248; forms of comparison, 87, 249; -ing verb form as, 251; position, 87–88, 248, *Exercises 89–94, 96, 99, 101, Pattern 107*
adverb clause, 246, 252, 266, *Patterns 133, 135, 147*
adverb phrase, 250
adverbial conjunction, 266–67, *Patterns 141, 142*
agreement, 3–26, 209; pronoun and antecedent, 5–6, 59, *Exercises 19, 25, 77;* subject and verb, 3–5, 209, *Exercises 7–18, 21–25*
antecedent, 5–6, 59, 226, *Exercises 19, 23, 25, 59, 77*
apostrophe, 59, 225, *Patterns 107, 110, 111, 119*
appositive, 58, 235, *Exercise 73, Patterns 113, 115*
auxiliary, 27–30, 206
auxiliary equivalent, 208

b

be, 27, 213–14, *Exercise 35*
begin, 28, *Exercise 41*
broad reference of pronoun, 6, 226

c

case, 57–59, 228, *Exercises 61–76, 79–86*
clause: adjective, 252, 266; adverb, 266, *Patterns 133, 135;* defined, 237; elliptical, 252, 266, *Patterns 133, 135;* main, 265–66, *Patterns 137, 139, 140, 141, 143, 144, 145, 147, 149;* noun, 237, *Patterns 122, 123, 150, 181;* parenthetical, 254, *Pattern 137;* subordinate, 237, *Patterns 140, 147, 149, 151*
colon, *Patterns 140, 150*
come, 29, *Exercise 43*
comma: adverbial conjunction, 266–67, *Patterns 141, 142;* appositive, *Patterns 113, 115;* correlative comparative, 249; direct address, 238–39; introductory elements, 266, *Patterns 133, 135, 147, 150, 173, 179;* main clauses joined by *and, but,* etc., *Patterns 143, 144, 145;* nominative absolute, *Patterns 139, 140;* nonrestrictive elements, 254, 266, *Patterns 113, 132, 133, 135, 147, 173, 179;* showing omission, *Pattern 175;* parenthetical elements, *Patterns 137, 139, 142, 150, 161, 163;* quotations, *Patterns 130, 131;* series, *Patterns 150, 159, 165, 167;* transitional expressions, 255, 267, *Pattern 177*
comparison, 87, 249
complement: object, 57, 232–33; subject, 57, 87, 213, 231; verbal, 58, 234
complex sentence, 265, *Patterns 132, 147, 150, 151, 173, 177, 183*
compound noun, 223–24; compound pronoun, 226
compound sentence, 266, *Patterns 141, 142, 143, 147, 153, 155, 175, 177, 183*
compound subject, 4
compound-complex sentence, *Pattern 181*
conjugation, 208, 209, 213
conjunction: adverbial, 266–67; coordinating, 264, 265; correlative, 265; relater, 263–67; subordinating, 252, 265–66, *Patterns 141, 142, 144, 145, 147*

conjunctive adverb: see *adverbial conjunction*

contractions, 59, 228

coordinating conjunctions, or coordinators: 264–65, *Patterns 144, 145, 147*

correlative comparative, 249

correlative conjunction, 265

d

-d or -ed verbs, 27, 211–12, *Exercises 31–33*

dash, *Patterns 153, 155, 157, 159, 161*

degrees of comparison, 87, 249

demonstrative pronoun, 226

dependent clause: see *subordinate clause*

developing the paragraph: see *paragraph*

direct address, 238–39

direct object: see *object*

direct question, *Patterns 125, 127, 157, 165*

direct quotation, *Patterns 129, 130, 131*

divided quotation, *Pattern 131*

do, 28, *Exercise 40*

drink, 28, *Exercise 41*

e

elliptical elements, 252, 266

equivalents: adverb, 248; auxiliary, 208; verb, 207

exclamations, *Patterns 127, 157*

expletive: defined, 268; position, 4–5, 231, 268, *Exercise 13, Patterns 121, 123, 151*

eye-passive, 214

f

form changes: 3–100; adjective, 87, 249; adverb, 87, 249; noun, 3, 210, 224–25; pronoun, 57–59, 227–28; verb 3–5, 27–29, 206, 208, 210

formal usage: expletive *there*, 5; pronoun subject complement, 57; reference of pronouns, 59; subjunctive, 217; superlative, 87; *who* and *whom*, 57, *Exercise 67*

fragment, 205, *Exercise 35*

functional shift, 247, 248, 262, 264, 268

future tense, 209

g

gerund, 59, 229, *Exercises 75, 79, 83, Patterns 117, 119*

get, 28

go, 28, *Exercise 40*

grammar, 205–71

h

has, have, and *had,* 27–29

helping verb: see *auxiliary*

hyphen, 252–53, *Patterns 108, 109*

i

imperative, 215, *Pattern 144*

implicit passive, 215, 251

indefinite pronouns, 3–5, 59, 226

independent clause: see *main clause*

indicative mood, 30, 215, 216

indirect object: see *object*

indirect question, *Patterns 125, 127, 165*

indirect quotation, *Patterns 129, 130, 131*

infinitive: bare, 230; defined, 210–11, 229–30; as form of verb, 27–29; as modifier, 251; as noun, 230; pronouns with, 58, 234; sign of, 230; subject of, 58, 235, *Patterns 117, 119, 121, 122, 167*

inflection: see *form changes*

informal usage: expletive *there,* 5; pronoun subject complement, 57; reference of pronouns, 59; subjunctive, 217; superlative, 87; *who,* 57, *Exercise 67*

-*ing* verbs, 27, 211

interrupters, *Patterns 157, 161*

irregular comparison, 249

irregular verbs: conjugation of *be,* 213; defined, 212; list of, 28–29, *Exercises 35–47*

it as expletive, 231, 268, *Patterns 121, 123, 151*

l

lay, lie, 29, *Exercises 45, 47*

linking verb, 87, 213

loose sentence, *Pattern 173*

-*ly,* 87, 248

m

main clause, 265–66, *Patterns 137, 139, 140, 141, 143, 144, 145, 147, 149*
markers: infinitive, 230; noun, 223
modifiers: 87–102, 245–55; adjective, 87, 213, 247–49; adverb, 87–88, 248–49, 251; clause, 246, 252, 254; comparison, 87–89; defined, 245; hyphenated, 252–53, *Patterns 108, 109;* nonrestrictive or parenthetical, 254; phrase, 88, 246, 250, 251, 253; position, 88, 253; single-word, 88, 246, *Exercises 89–102, Patterns 105, 107–11, 113, 132, 133, 135, 147, 163, 167*
mood: 30, 215; imperative, 215, *Pattern 144;* indicative, 30, 215, 216; subjunctive, 30, 216, *Exercise 49, Pattern 135*

n

-*n* and -*en* verbs, 28, *Exercise 37*
nominative absolute, 238, *Patterns 139, 140*
nominative case, 228
nonrestrictive adjective clauses, 254, *Patterns 113, 132*
nonsentence, 205
noun: 223–44; appositives, 235; compound, 223–24; defined, 223; direct address, 239; form changes, 3, 210, 224–25; markers, 223; nominative absolute, noun-centered expression, 238; number, 3, 224; objects, 232–34; phrases, 236; possessive, 225; subject complements, 231; subjects, 3–5, 230; suffixes, 223, *Patterns 109, 110, 111, 122, 123, 150, 181*
noun clause, 237, *Patterns 122, 123, 150, 181*
noun substitutes, 226–38; appositives, 235; clauses, 237; gerunds, 229; direct address, 238; infinitives, 230; objects, 232–33; phrases, 236; pronouns, 59, 226–28; subject complements, 231; subjects, 230; with verbals, 234
number, 3–26, 209–10; nouns, 3, 224; pronouns, 3–6, 227, *Exercises 7–26*

o

object forms of pronouns, 57–58, 228, *Exercises 9, 55, 65, 67, 69, 71, 73, 81, 85*

objective case, 228
objects: defined, 232; noun substitutes, 232–33; of prepositions, 3, 57–58, 233, 261–62, *Pattern 179;* of verbals, 58, 234, *Exercise 69;* of verbs, 57, 232, 233, *Pattern 179*
omission shown by comma, *Pattern 175*

p

paragraph: 187–222; analysis, 201; argument, 193; arrangement of details, 196, 197, 198; character sketch, 189; classification, 200; clincher sentence, 188, 194; comparison, contrast, 188, 189, 191, 199; definition, 190; description, 187–88, 188–89, 191, 194, 195–96; example, 190, 195; explanation, 188, 190; images, 188–89; incident, 192, 197–98; instruction, 198; point of view, 189; reasons, 195; specific details, 187, 188, 189, 191, 192, 196, 199; "strawman," 193; surprise ending, 197–98; unity, 187
parallelism, *Patterns 159, 165, 167, 169*
parentheses, *Pattern 155*
parenthetical elements: adverbial conjunction, 266–67, *Patterns 141, 142;* clause, 254, 266, *Patterns 113, 132, 133, 137;* direct address, 238, 239; phrase, 97, 238, *Patterns 139, 140, 150, 161, 163, 167, 173*
participial phrase, 88, 251, *Exercise 97, Patterns 105, 108, 163, 167*
participle, 27–30, 88, 211, 229, 251
passive voice, 27, 214; eye-passive, 214; *get,* 28; implicit, 215, 251
past participle, 27–30, 211
past tense, 27, 211
perfect tense, 213
periodic sentence, *Pattern 173*
person, 3, 209, 210
personal pronouns, 57–59, 226–28
phrases: absolute, 238; adjective and adverb, 250; defined, 236; gerund, 59, 229; infinitive, 229–30, 251; noun, 236; noun substitutes, 236; participial, 88, 251; prepositional, 57–58, 250; verb, 27, 206
plural: figures, 225; nouns, 3, 224; pronouns, 3–6, 227; symbols, 225
positive degree of comparison, 87, 249

possessive case, 59, 225, 228, *Exercises 75, 79, 83, Patterns 110, 111, 119*

postponed subject, 268

predicate: see *verb*

predicate adjective, predicate nominative: see *subject complement*

preposition: defined, 261; ending sentence, 233; list of, 262; object of, 3, 57–58, 233, 261–62, *Pattern 179*

prepositional phrase, 57–58; as modifier, 250; as noun, 236, *Exercise 9, Patterns 107, 109, 111, 149, 161*

present participle, 29, 211

present tense, 3, 209

principal verbs, 28–29, 206

progressive form of verbs, 27, 211

pronoun: antecedent, 5–6, 59, 226; appositive, 58; case, 57–59, 228; compound, 226; defined, 226; demonstrative, 226; form changes, 57–59, 227, 228; indefinite, 3–5, 59, 226; with infinitives, 58, 234, *Exercises 9, 55, 61–86;* nominative case, 228; number, 3–6, 227; object forms, 57–58, 228; objective case, 228; personal, 57–59, 226, 228; possessive, 59, 228; reference, 5–6, 59, 226; relative, 5, 226, 228, 263; subject forms, 3, 57, 228; after *than* and *as,* 58

punctuation: apostrophe, 59, 225, *Patterns 107, 110, 111, 119;* colon, *Patterns 140, 150;* comma, 238–39, 249, 254, 255, 266–67, *Patterns 113, 115, 130–35, 137, 139, 141–45, 147, 150, 159, 161, 163, 165, 167, 173, 175, 177, 179;* dash, *Patterns 153, 155, 157, 159, 161;* exclamation point, *Patterns 127, 157;* hyphen, 252, 253, *Patterns 108, 109;* parentheses, *Pattern 155;* question mark, *Patterns 125, 127, 157, 165;* quotation marks, *Patterns 129, 130, 131;* semicolon, 267, *Patterns 137, 139, 141, 175, 181*

q

question, direct and indirect, *Patterns 125, 127, 157, 165*

quotation: direct, *Patterns 129, 130, 131;* divided, *Pattern 131;* indirect, *Pattern 129, 130, 131*

quotation marks, *Patterns 129, 130, 131*

r

reference of pronouns, 5–6, 59, 226

regular comparison, 249

regular verb, 27, 211–12, *Exercises 31–33*

relative pronoun, 5, 228, 263, 266, *Exercises 15, 17*

relaters, 261–67; conjunctions, 252, 263–67; defined, 261; prepositions, 263, *Patterns 141, 142, 144, 145, 147*

restrictive adjective clause, 254

run, 29, *Exercise 43*

s

see, 28, *Exercise 40*

semicolon, 267, *Patterns 137, 139, 141, 175, 181*

sentence: complex, 265, *Patterns 132, 147, 150, 151, 173, 177, 183;* compound, 266, *Patterns 141, 142, 143, 147, 153, 155, 175, 177, 183;* compound-complex, *Pattern 181;* defined, 205; distinguished from fragment, 205, *Exercise 35;* exclamatory, *Patterns 127, 157;* imperative, 215, *Pattern 144;* interrogative, *Patterns 125, 127, 157, 165;* loose, *Pattern 173;* periodic, *Pattern 173;* simple, 265, *Patterns 132, 141, 142, 143, 149, 150, 151, 153, 155, 159, 161, 163, 165, 167, 169, 171, 179, 181, 183*

series, *Patterns 150, 159, 165, 167*

set, 29, *Exercise 45*

shift, functional, 247, 248, 262, 264, 268

simple past tense, 27, 211

simple sentence, 265–66; see *sentence*

singular number, 3–5, 59

sit, 29, *Exercise 47*

subject: agreement with verb, 3–5, 209; compound, 4; delayed, *Patterns 121, 123;* forms, 57–58; of infinitive, 58, 235; noun substitutes, 230; number, 3–5, 209; position, 5, 231; postponed, 268, *Pattern 121, 123;* pronoun, 3, 4, 57

subject complement, 57, 87, 213, 231

subject forms of pronouns, 3, 57, 58, 228

subjunctive mood, 30, 216, *Exercise 49, Pattern 135*

subordinate clause, 237; adjective, 252; adverb, 252, 266; defined, 237; noun, 237–38; relationship to main clause, 238, 265 subordinating conjunctions, or subordinators, 252, 265–66, *Patterns 144, 145*

superlative degree of comparison, 87, 249

supposed to, 27, *Exercise 31*

swim, 28, *Exercise 41*

t

tense, 27–30, 209, 211

there as expletive, 4–5, 268, *Exercise 13, Pattern 151*

topics for composition, 187–201

transitional expressions, 255, 267, *Pattern 177*

u

understood subject, 215, *Pattern 144*

usage, formal and informal: expletive *there,* 5; pronoun subject complement, 57; reference of pronouns, 59; subjunctive, 217; superlative, 87; *who* and *whom,* 57, *Exercise 67*

used to, 27, *Exercise 31*

v

verb equivalent, 207

verbal, 229

verbs: action, 87, 232–33; active voice, 29, 214; agreement with subject, 3–5, 209; auxiliary, 27–30, 206; auxiliary equivalent, 208; basic forms, 210; conjugation, 208; defined, 205; equivalents, 207; form changes, 3–5, 27–29, 206, 208, 210; helpers, 27–30, 206, 208; infinitive form, 27–29, 210–11; *-ing* verb, 27, 211; irregular, 28–29, 212–13, *Exercises 35–47;* linking, 87, 213; mood, 30, 215–16; objects of, 57, 232, 233; passive voice, 27–29, 214; phrase, 206; position, 205; principal parts, 210; progressive, 27, 211; regular, 27, 211–12; subjunctive, 30, 216; tense, 3, 28–29, 209; voice, 27–29, 214, *Exercises 7–18, 21–25, 31–56*

voice: active, 29, 214, *Pattern 177;* passive, 27–29, 214–15, 251

w

who, whom 57, *Exercises 67, 81*